HIS PART AND OURS

THE BOOKS OF J. SIDLOW BAXTER

AWAKE, MY HEART
Daily devotional meditations for the entire year. These readings are "beautifully simple and simply beautiful, profoundly simple and simply profound." — *Evangelical Christian*

GOING DEEPER
A deeply spiritual study on the theme of knowing, loving and serving our Lord Jesus Christ.

HIS PART AND OURS
Enriching exposition and devotional studies in the reciprocal union of Christ and His people. "A truly great book."
— *Moody Monthly*

GOD SO LOVED
A captivating new presentation of John 3:16. Theological, devotional, practical. In two parts — (1) The New Testament Truth, (2) The Old Testament Type.

STUDIES IN PROBLEM TEXTS
Informing, elucidatory and applicatory expositions of certain Scripture passages which have occasioned perplexity.

MARK THESE MEN
Arresting studies in striking aspects of Bible characters with special relevances for our own times and the days ahead.

EXPLORE THE BOOK
A notable work on the Bible; in one handsome volume of approximately 1800 pages, 6 volumes in one.

THE STRATEGIC GRASP OF THE BIBLE
A series of studies in the structural and dispensational characteristics of the Bible.

HIS PART AND OURS

God's Promises
and Our Responsibilities
in the Christian Life

J. SIDLOW BAXTER

ZONDERVAN
PUBLISHING HOUSE   OF THE ZONDERVAN CORPORATION
GRAND RAPIDS, MICHIGAN 49506

First printing	1960
Second printing	1962
Third printing	1964
Fourth printing	1967
Fifth printing	1969
Sixth printing	1970
Seventh printing	1971
Eighth printing	1972
Ninth printing	1974

Printed in the United States of America

FOREWORD

SIMPLICITY is aimed at in these pages. To few men is it given to be profound or original. Simplicity is open to all. Moreover, the author believes that most human hearts are helped far more by the simple than the profound.

Yet, in the final analysis, what *is* profundity, and what simplicity? It is a true paradox (and a very comforting one to some of us) that the really profound is often the most simple, and the simple the most truly profound. This much we may certainly say, that while the treatment of the truths dealt with in these pages is designedly simple, the truths themselves are profound and vital, and pricelessly precious to the people of Christ.

These messages were first delivered in the ordinary course of the author's ministry at Charlotte Chapel, Edinburgh; and grateful acknowledgment is due in respect of encouraging words spoken by appreciative hearers. The discourses are here reproduced almost verbatim. May many a believer find comfort in them now that they are committed to this more permanent form!—and to the dear Saviour be all the praise.

J. S. B.

DEDICATION

Synchronizing with the publication of this little book is the seventieth birthday of my dear mother. This is a truly auspicious event, not only to herself, but also to her children. If ever a man had cause to bless God for "a mother in a thousand," I have. It was at her knee that I first learned "the story of Jesus and His love." It was in her that I first saw something of what Jesus can be to a human heart. It was by her wise counsels that I was forearmed in days of youth. From my infancy her prayers have enwrapped me like invisible garments. This little book is unpretentious enough in itself, but if it were ten times bigger and better it could not convey more affection; and, with unspeakable gratitude to God, I here dedicate it to that noble, godly woman whom, in His loving kindness, He gave to be

MY MOTHER

CONTENTS

"*HIS* PART"

"*OUR* PART"

CONTENTS

A PRAYER

Part One

—"*HIS* PART"

All the good things that can be reckoned up here below have only a finite and limited goodness. Some can clothe but cannot feed; others can nourish but cannot secure; others adorn but cannot advance; all do serve but none do satisfy. They are like a beggar's coat made up of many pieces, not all enough either to beautify or defend. But Christ is full and sufficient for all His people: righteousness to cover all their sins, plenty enough to supply all their wants, grace enough to subdue all their lusts, wisdom enough to vanquish all their enemies, virtue enough to cure all their diseases, fulness enough to save them to the utmost. He is bread, wine, milk, living waters, to feed them; He is a garment of righteousness to cover and adorn them; a Physician to heal them; a Counsellor to advise them; a Captain to defend them; a Prince to rule; a Prophet to teach; a Priest to make atonement for them; a Husband to protect; a Father to provide; a Brother to relieve; a Foundation to support; a Root to quicken; a Head to guide; a Treasure to enrich; a Sun to enlighten; and a Fountain to cleanse; so that as the one ocean hath more waters than all the rivers of the world, and one sun more light than all the luminaries in heaven, so one Christ is more to a poor soul than if it had all the world a thousand times over.
—JOHN SPENCER.

MY GRACE

" He said unto me: My grace is sufficient for thee."—2 Cor. xii. 9.

PAUL had a "thorn" in the flesh. Was he alone in this? Saints, apostles, prophets, martyrs, answer "No." There is a thorn in every life. There is a cross even in the heart of God. The Saviour must wear a *crown* of thorns; and what was that thorny wreath but the symbol of those jagged thorns which tore His soul?

There is no song that human hearts are singing but has some note of haunting sadness. There is no rose of summer's bringing but has some thorn unseen amid its leaves. There is no garden but some weed encloses. There is no day but has its hour of pain. There are no eyes but sometime have been blinded by silent tears of pity or of grief. There is no life which has not held some sorrow. There is no soul but has its secret strife. There is no sky, however clear and beaming, but holds the hidden vapour of some cloud.

It belongs to our peace to become gratefully reconciled to the presence of this seeming jar in the present running of things. Down through the years, thoughtful minds have become more and more persuaded that pain has a noble part in the plan. Suffering has made saints. Pain has matured character. Many a man who has cursed a blind fate for some ugly thorn that has ripped his heart has discovered the true God through his calamity, and afterwards given thanks in truer language for a gracious chastisement that saved his soul. God knows how foolishly our weak hearts cling to the seeming instead of the real; and it is well that we should learn to sing, with Adelaide Proctor,

> I thank Thee, Lord, that all our joy
> Is touched with pain;
> That shadows fall on brightest hours,
> That thorns remain:
> So that earth's bliss may be our guide,
> And not our chain.

What Paul's thorn was is not explicitly divulged. Scripture exercises kind reserve here, so that *all* who are afflicted, however differently from Paul, may share in the Divine comfort which came to him. The Scriptures are as wise in their reservations as in their revelations. Enough is revealed to make faith intelligent. Enough is reserved to give faith scope for development.

Paul begged that his thorn might be removed. He thought it exceptionally grievous. We each think our own is worse than any other. There is no hint that Paul complained. He *prayed*. Affliction should drive us *to* God, not *from* Him. If praying preceded complaining, how often would we bless rather than blame!

Paul's prayer was definite and repeated. He says: "For *this thing* I besought the Lord *thrice*, that it might depart from me." Some pray for everything in general and get nothing in particular. Others call upon God but do not stay at Heaven's gate until the answer comes. Not so with Paul: his cry is urgent and persistent. As in the garden the Lord Himself thrice uttered His agonizing prayer, so now the apostle, with sweat of anguish on his brow, three times implores that "this thing" may be taken away. Yet as the "cup" could not pass from Christ, so the "thorn" was not removed from Paul.

Paul's prayer, then, was not answered? No! Yes! Which? Both. It was really and gloriously answered, not according to "the letter," it is true, but spiritually, and in a way which brought blessing otherwise impossible, both to himself and millions of others. "He said unto me: My grace is sufficient for thee."

"*He said* unto me"—the Risen One speaks directly to His tested servant. Beautiful evidence of Christ's tender concern! There have been times, perhaps, when some dire agony has wrung from our hearts the cry, "Does Jesus care? Why has this trouble come? Why is it not removed? Why is prayer not answered?"

> Does Jesus care when my heart is pained
>   Too deeply for mirth or song?
> When for my deep grief I find no relief,
>   Though my tears flow all the night long?

Does Jesus really know and feel and care at such times?

Let the risen Saviour's personal assurance to Paul be a heartening guarantee that He does indeed care. He is "touched with the feeling of our infirmity."

"He said *unto me*"—perhaps no verse of Scripture has brought more comfort to Christian hearts than this one; and does not the explanation of its pre-eminent appeal largely lie in the fact that it is the record of a personal experience? "He said unto *me*." There is an instinctive persuasion in the human heart that the experience of one is realizable by another. That is why the testifying of the Lord's people among themselves and to others is important. Maybe we do not have enough old-fashioned "testimony meetings" in our churches to-day!

"My grace is sufficient for thee"—sublime and satisfying answer! How much better than the literal granting of the apostle's request! Had the pleading of those sensitive nerves been literally yielded to, what losers would Paul and ourselves have been! Paul would have lost more power than pain; and how many thoughts that have since inspired patient heroism would never have come to us! Such epistles as Paul's could only have their birth in the travail of trial. Paul's prayer was sincere and intense, but it left the higher spiritual altitudes unscaled. To have the thorn removed was poor compared with having its presence sanctified. To have the "messenger of Satan" taken away was poor compared with having him transformed into a "ministering spirit." Paul wanted the thorn away; whereas Christ wanted to show how grapes may be gathered of thorns. God's choicest flowers often bloom on bitter stems. "No chastening for the present seemeth to be joyous, but grievous; nevertheless afterward it yieldeth fruit."

"My grace is sufficient for thee"—it is a true paradox that God sometimes answers our prayers by not answering them. He "reads between the lines" and sees the thing that is bigger than our words. Monica begs God that her son may not go to Rome, with all its temptations; yet God allows him to go; and there, in the very place which has been dreaded, young Augustine is converted to Christ. The smaller prayer is ungranted that the larger yearning and purpose may be fulfilled. Paul himself came to see that what at first looked like a refusal was in reality the wisest and grandest of all answers. Indeed, as Dr. James Denney says, "A refusal *is* an answer if it is so

given that God and the soul henceforth understand one another." God may not always grant the spoken wish, but He will never withhold that which we need. God not only grants prayers; He guides lives.

"*My* grace"—how gloriously the grace of Christ shines from the pages of the New Testament! Gaze at that matchless character. See His perfect grace revealing itself through everything He said and did, giving Him perfect poise in every situation and on all occasions. See how He combines in Himself all the masculine virtues and all the feminine graces. Gaze at Calvary. See that utter triumph of sheer self-sacrifice! O that life! that death! "We beheld His glory, the glory as of the Only Begotten of the Father, *full of grace and truth.*" That grace, both by imputation and impartation, may be *mine*!

"*My* grace"—who but the absolutely Divine Christ could say this? What mere creature would *presume* to say this? How empty would the words be from the lips of any but a Christ who is verily God! "*My* grace"—the words involve omnipotence, omniscience, omnipresence, the possession of all the Divine resources, the perfect knowledge of all human needs, and Christ's perpetual presence everywhere with His people. For any mere creature to make such a claim—whether worm or archangel makes no essential difference—would be both ludicrous and blasphemous. Yet the Lord Jesus utters the promise with perfect propriety: and in this we see one of the many incidental implications of Christ's deity which are scattered throughout the New Testament. Christ is God in the absolute sense of the word. His grace is exhaustless as Himself, absolutely adequate, infallibly unfailing. Divine grace in all its fullness, freshness, and freeness, gushes to us from that precious pronoun "My."

"*Sufficient*"—the supply has exact correspondence with the need; never too much, never too little, but perfect adequacy: never too soon, never too late, but timed to the tick of the clock and to the beat of the heart. Grace for to-morrow's needs will not come to-day. Grace for to-day will not come to-morrow. There is a story comes to us from the old-time martyr days, about a condemned Christian who lay one night in his prison cell knowing that at daybreak he must be burned at the stake. The prospect was terrible. How could he endure the ordeal? He picked up the candle that flickered in his cell, and tried the experiment of holding his little finger in the tiny flame. With a gasp of pain he quickly withdrew it. How could he possibly undergo the torture of his whole body given to the flames? Yet at sunrise he went to his death with irrepressible exuberance. Amid the circling flames he testified to the all-sufficient grace of Christ, and sang with a heavenly ecstasy shining from his face. When the real emergency came sufficient grace was given to make him "more than conqueror." So is it always. "Sufficient unto the day is the evil thereof"—and sufficient unto the evil is the grace!

"*Sufficient*"—Divine grace is infinite and exhaustless, but it is never dispensed superfluously. We must not expect that grace will be given for the doing of the needless. There are some Christians who stir up needless opposition to themselves and then think they are the Lord's special heroes because they have to suffer. We should guard against this. Grace is only promised for real need. God does not give grace for the spectacular heroism of public martyrdom to one who is called to keep an office ledger. He gives grace to that one to keep patient and gracious amid the tediousness of the office routine. Somebody once asked D. L. Moody, "Have you grace enough to be burned at the stake?" Mr. Moody replied, "No." The questioner pressed him further, "Do you not wish you had?" "No," replied Moody again, "for I do not need it. What I need just now is grace to live in Milwaukee three days and hold a mission."

> My Lord has never said that He would give
>   Another's grace without another's thorn:
> What matter, since for every day of mine
>   Sufficient grace for me comes with the morn?
>
> And though the future brings some heavier cross,
>   I need not cloud the present with my fears:
> I know the grace that is enough to-day
>   Will be sufficient still through all the years.

"*Sufficient*"—the grace of Christ is *always and evermore* sufficient. See that noble, rolling river; it has been flowing for thousands of years, watering the fields, and slaking the thirst of a hundred generations; yet it shows no sign of exhaustion. See the morning sun as he shoots his golden arrows high above

the mountain crests, and as he gilds the curtains of the dawn
with a glittering glory. He has been performing this daily miracle
for millenniums; he has melted the snows of six thousand
winters, and renewed the verdure of as many summers; yet
he shines as gloriously as ever; his eye is not dimmed, and his
natural strength is unabated. Gaze out across the heaving
bosom of the ocean, greater than all the earth's rivers in one.
For ages it has rolled its tides around the globe and washed the
shores of the five continents; yet its mighty volumes are as deep
and full as ever; its tossing tides rush in, as fresh and exhilar-
ating as in the days of the race's infancy. Do not these things
try to speak to us of the grace of Christ? In Him are fountains
that never run dry, and rivers that never cease their flowing.
He is a sun that never languishes, and an ocean ever full.
Certainly indeed is His grace "sufficient" for us. His "sufficiency" is simply the expression *toward us* of His infinite fullness.

"*For thee.*" A bygone preacher has reverently dared the
remark that there is a touch of beautiful ludicrousness in this
text, in the contrast between the first word and the last.
"*My* grace"—there is the absolutely infinite. "For *thee*"—
there is the comparatively infinitesimal. As though the mighty
ocean should say to the wee laddie playing on the sands,
"Little boy, my ocean depths are sufficient to fill your bucket."
As though a vast cornfield should say to a solitary mouse,
"Little one, my great harvest is enough to feed you." As
though a man standing on some high summit should say, "I
must not breathe too deeply lest I exhaust the atmosphere."
As though a tiny fish swimming in the Amazon should say, "I
must not drink too much water lest I drain the river." Have no
fear, burdened Christian, His grace is sufficient for *thee*!

"*For thee*"—not just for this present trial of yours, but for
you yourself, making you equal to *all* the trials that come. See
here the Divine method with us. God does not pledge Himself
to be ever altering our circumstances and removing our burdens
in answer to our prayers. Our truest blessings often come
through the things that seem most grievous to us. If God were
always levelling down our circumstances to our spiritual condition we should waste away with spiritual dry-rot. It would
be with us as it was with the old-time Hebrews: "He gave them
their request but sent leanness into their soul." Christ's way is

to make *us* equal to our circumstances rather than reduce our circumstances to what *we* short-sightedly think they ought to be. Dr. Phillips Brooks has a forceful word to this effect: "Do not pray for easy lives! Pray to be stronger men. Do not pray for tasks equal to your powers. Pray for powers equal to your tasks. Then the doing of your work shall be no miracle. But *you* shall be a miracle. Every day you shall wonder at yourself, at the richness of life which has come to you by the grace of God."

"*For thee.*" Thorns and trials are blessings indeed if they bring the opportunity for the grace of Christ to perfect *our character*. Some flowers, as the rose, must be crushed ere their full fragrance is released. Some fruit, as the sycamore, must be bruised before it will attain ripeness and sweetness. Some metals, as gold, must be flung into the furnace before they reach full value and purity. The old oak log must be laid on the fire, and the flames encircle it, before its imprisoned music is set free. So is it often with the saints. It is true with many of us that we must be laid low before we will look high. We must know God's smiting before we can appreciate His smiling. The potter must break the vessel ere he can make out of the same material a new and beautiful vase. Our hearts must be broken before their richest contents can leak out and flow forth to bless others. Whenever God sends a trial with one hand, He gives grace with the other. Thus trials become triumphs. Burdens become wings. Affliction, instead of being a bed of thorns and a pathway of nettles, becomes a quilt of roses. The very things which seem to break us are the things which really make us. Euroclydon blows its tempests upon us! We shall be dashed in pieces on the rock-bound coast! We shall be strangled in the hidden reef! But nay, we are self-deceived. Lo, God is in the hurricane, and instead of driving the scared mariner to destruction it beats him into that safest of all harbours, the encircling arms of the Divine love. Yea, it is so; trials, tribulations, adversities, are often our biggest benedictions; blessings in disguise; angels garbed in black for a small moment; messengers from heaven, come to make us more like the Captain of our salvation who Himself was made "perfect through sufferings." The thorny crown was in the plan for Jesus; but the thorns have given place to diadems! The cross was the step to the throne. "My grace is sufficient *for thee*." "It is God Who worketh *in you* both to will and to do of His good pleasure." However jagged the thorn, it is a blessing if it bleeds away our selfishness.

"*For thee*." Underneath all our care is Christ's care for *us*. Henry Moorhouse returned home one morning, carrying a parcel, a present for his wife, and was greeted by his lame daughter who asked that she might have the pleasure of taking the present to the room where mother was. "But you know, dear, that *you* cannot carry it," he said, thinking of her lameness. "Give it me, and see," she challenged him. So the parcel was handed to her, and then she said, "Now *I'll* carry the parcel, and you carry *me*!" So is it with ourselves. If I must carry a burden, Christ will carry *me*. Underneath us are the everlasting arms of an all-sufficient grace which never fails. Grace is imparted at every step of the way; grace for the big things and grace for the little things.

> His grace is great enough to meet the great things,
>> The crashing waves that overwhelm the soul,
> The roaring winds that leave us stunned and breathless,
>> The sudden storms beyond our life's control.
> His grace is great enough to meet the small things,
>> The little pin-prick troubles that annoy,
> The insect worries, buzzing and persistent,
>> The squeaking wheels that grate upon our joy.

"*My grace is sufficient for thee*." Oh, what a wondrous promise this is! The more one thinks upon it the more glorious it becomes. We are such unutterably needy creatures that only God Himself can know the measure of our need; and God Himself, in Christ Jesus, pledges to meet us at every point of our need. The promise is in the present tense: "My grace *IS* sufficient." His grace is sufficient *now*. I need grace for each moment as it comes, and His grace is constant as my breathing.

> Grace when the sun is shining, Lord,
>> Grace when the sky is black,
> Grace when I get the unkind word,
>> Grace on the too smooth track,
> Grace when I'm elbowed into a nook,
>> Grace when I get *my* turn,
> Grace when the dinner will not cook,
>> Grace when the fire won't burn.

Grace when my duties all go wrong,
 Grace when they all go right,
Grace when it's gladness, praise, and song,
 Grace when I have to fight,
Grace when my clothes are fresh and new,
 Grace when they're old and dull,
Grace when my purse is empty too,
 Grace when it's over-full.

Grace when the saved ones don't *act* saved,
 Grace when they all blame me,
Grace when denied the good I've craved,
 Grace when I'm giv'n my plea,
Grace when the midnight hours I tell,
 Grace when the morn is nigh,
Grace when I'm healthy, strong, and well,
 Grace when I come to die.

"*My grace is sufficient for thee.*" Is the grace of Christ *really* adequate in the extreme adversities of human experience? Let us see. Take the following couple of examples, picked from many which might be given.

Here is a letter from a missionary. "On my arrival from China, I received a letter asking me to call and see an invalid. I knew he was blind, but I was not prepared to see what I did see. He was lying upon the bed, every joint in his body immovable, unable to turn in any direction. But his mind was full of vigour, his heart full of the grace of service. For twenty-nine years he has lain thus, fed only on liquid foods. For twenty-two years he has been blind. Is it possible that such a one as he could do anything to help others? Listen : seventeen blind children are supported by his efforts, in India ; ten in China ; a blind Bible-woman in Korea ; a blind boy in the Sudan ; a blind boy in Fiji ; a blind Bible-woman in Jaffa. Three hundred pounds a year is received in answer to prayer by that faithful, sightless, silent, paralysed disciple in that little shut-in room in Melbourne." Yes, "My grace is sufficient for thee!"

Miss E. Wakefield MacGill, of the Pocket Testament League, was staying at my home recently, and told me the following remarkable story. Years ago, when her devout and gifted father was superintendent of a Gospel Mission in Glasgow, there was a great deal of trouble caused by a gang of young fellows, in a slummy part of Glasgow, who were set on all kinds of mischief and violence. Even the police found it necessary to go in pairs or trios round the locality. The gang of young ruffians drank and gambled and fought and plotted and thieved and, among other things, determined to smash up the revival which had broken out at the Gospel Mission under Mr. MacGill's faithful preaching. The results, however, turned out the very opposite of what they anticipated. When some of them came as spies to the meetings, they fell under the power of the Gospel and were either soundly converted to Christ or at least deeply convicted by the Holy Spirit. In the end, every one of those godless young roughs and criminals—a dozen or more in all—fell prey to Jesus and became saved.

This happened some twenty-five or thirty years before Miss MacGill's recent visit to my home in Edinburgh; and, gradually with the lapse of years, all those young terrorists, after being soundly saved, had become widely scattered from each other. But after all those years there comes to light at least one cheering and touching sequel, quite by coincidence. Two men, seeing Miss MacGill's name advertised in connection with the recent meeting which she was to address in Edinburgh, found a flood of memories pouring into their minds at the sight of that name, "MacGill," and, all unknown to each other, decided to attend the meeting. These two men had both been members of that Glasgow gang years before, and had never once seen each other through all the intervening years. They recognized each other in the meeting, and the minute it was over they hastened to each other with unrestrainable eagerness. With much emotion they shook each other by the hand. "Charlie!" —"Jim!"—"Fancy, seeing you again after all these years!" Then Charlie said, "Yes, praise the Lord, I'm still going on in the Christian life; and from the day of my conversion nearly thirty years ago until this minute I've never once had any further taste for the wretched drink!" Jim's face clouded a bit at this, and a tear glistened in his eyes. "Well, Charlie," he said, "I'm afraid I canna' say that. I only wish I could. There's never been one single day through all these years that I haven't had the thirst for drink." And then he quickly added, "But, thank God, *I've never touched it from that day to this!*"

Now which of those two men had experienced the bigger victory? Which of the two had the greater testimony to the saving and keeping power of the Lord Jesus? Our Saviour has different ways with different natures and temperaments. He knows, far better than we ourselves do, what is most needful for us. In one case He plucks up some evil propensity by the very roots from the soil of our hearts, for He knows that such is the *only* way to set sin's prisoner free. In other cases He leaves the propensity there, for He sees that the fight against it is necessary to the growth of the soul and the development of strong Christian character. He is the absolute emancipator, but He is also the infallible psychologist. He reads us like an open book, and He knows what is wisest in each case. Personally, I think that the man who had never been liberated from the craving for drink, but who had lived in unbroken victory through nearly thirty years, was the greater victor of the two. What an exploit! And what a noble commentary on the Saviour's promise, "My grace is sufficient for thee"!

Many of ourselves, perhaps, could give glad testimony to the fact that our mighty Saviour has plucked out by the very roots certain inbred, evil proclivities of our nature over which we simply could never have gained victory. Yet there are other such propensities or weaknesses or temptations which He has allowed to stay with us despite our pleading prayers after weary battling. We must learn more fully to trust and prove His wisdom as well as His power. He knows us through and through, and, as His word says, "He will not suffer you to be tempted above that ye are able to bear." If our Saviour does not give us deliverance by some once-for-all elimination of a trouble, He will teach us the way of continuous victory through a moment-by-moment impartation of His all-sufficient grace. Anything which keeps us conscious of our own weakness and keeps us close to Christ is a sanctifying blessing. Our human extremity is our Lord's opportunity. We need not fear: He will never fail us; and if we keep our hearts open to the inflow of His grace we shall find that every day and for evermore it is enough. Fear not, then, tried and troubled believer, He has said it, and thousands have proved it—"My grace is sufficient for thee."

"*My grace is sufficient for thee.*" Look back again over the text. Here is the *source*—"MY grace." Here is the *supply*—

"SUFFICIENT." Here is the *sustenance* it brings—"Sufficient FOR THEE." The source is infinite. The supply is proportionate. The sustenance is individually adequate.

> He giveth more grace as the burdens grow greater,
>> He sendeth more strength as the labours increase.
> To added affliction He addeth His mercy,
>> To multiplied trials His multiplied peace.
> When we have exhausted our store of endurance,
>> When our strength has failed ere the day is half done,
> When we reach the end of our hoarded resources,
>> Our Father's full giving is only begun.
> His love has no limit, His grace has no measure,
>> His power no boundary known unto men;
> And out of His infinite riches in Jesus,
>> He giveth and giveth, and giveth again.

MY STRENGTH

The sharp agonies of our earthly life liberate the diviner life which is given us in Christ. It is in the extremity of mortal weakness that we become conscious of immortal strength. When the "outward man is decaying"—strength sinking, all earthly springs of delight running dry, human ties dissolving, darkness falling on our homes, friends failing us or passing into the unseen world, and leaving us lonely when most we need their support,—it is when the "outward man is decaying," through the loss of all the natural supplies of power and joy, that the "inward man" becomes vividly conscious that it is being "renewed day by day."—R. W. DALE.

The tears we shed are not in vain,
    Nor worthless is the heavy strife;
If, like the buried seed of grain,
    They rise to renovated life.
It is through tears our spirits grow;
    'Tis in the tempest souls expand,
If it but teaches us to go
    To Him Who holds it in His hand.
Oh, welcome, then, the stormy blast!
    Oh, welcome, then, the ocean's roar!
Ye only drive more sure and fast
    Our trembling bark to heaven's bright shore.
                                    T. C. UPHAM.

MY STRENGTH

"My strength is made perfect in weakness."—2 Cor. xii. 9.

To DIVORCE these words from their context is an unpardonable atrocity! They are the crux of the most touching piece of Pauline autobiography in the New Testament. It was from the lips of the ascended Christ Himself that the wonderful words were spoken—spoken to the pain-racked, stunned, and struggling apostle in the hour of his baffling extremity. "My grace is sufficient for thee; for My strength is made perfect in (thy) weakness." What an eye-opener! What a discovery! What an assurance! The words are the turning-point in a terrific battle. The banner that has been dragging on the ground is hoisted high aloft again ; and Paul breaks forth into a song of victory, "Most gladly therefore will I rather glory in my infirmities that the power of Christ may rest upon me!"

It will be well to read the words again in their setting. Having spoken of the wonderful revelations that were given to him when he was raptured to the third heaven, Paul continues as follows:

And lest I should be exalted above measure through the abundance of the revelations, there was given to me a thorn in the flesh, the messenger of Satan to buffet me, lest I should be exalted above measure. For this thing I besought the Lord thrice, that it might depart from me. And He said unto me: My grace is sufficient for thee; for My strength is made perfect in (thy) weakness. Most gladly therefore will I rather glory in my infirmities, that the power of Christ may rest upon me. Therefore I take pleasure in infirmities, in reproaches, in necessities, in persecutions, in distresses for Christ's sake; for when I am weak, then am I strong. —2 Cor. xii. 7-10.

In this passage there are some of the profoundest truths and most important spiritual lessons to be found in the Book of God. We point out just a few of them.

First, we see here *the danger of pride even in the ripest and deepest Christians.* Paul is about the last man whom we would have thought susceptible to the subtle pull of pride. From his writings and recorded conduct, subsequent to his conversion, we would have judged him to vie with Moses for meekness and humility. Besides, he had such a wonderful and mellowing spiritual experience, and was constrained by such a passionate love for Christ, that we would have thought pride to be not only intolerable, but well-nigh impossible to him. Yet it is Paul himself who says, twice over, in this brief passage, "Lest I should be exalted above measure . . . lest I should be exalted above measure"! What a warning! Do we not need to heed it? The original idea in the putting of weather-cocks at the top of church steeples was to remind people that even Peter, the first among the apostles, fell into deep and grievous sin, and was denying his Lord when the cock crew long ago. The higher we rise, the further we may fall! Lucifer was the highest among the high, and he falls to the bottomless abyss! The most vehement Divine denunciations in Scripture are against pride! A thousand warnings and assurances are summed up in that one verse, "God resisteth the proud but giveth grace to the humble." Therefore "let him that thinketh he standeth take heed lest he fall."

A second lesson in this passage is that *temptations to pride may lurk in the least likely places.* Our highest privileges may become a subtle inducement to conceit. Paul had been the supremely honoured recipient of most wonderful Divine communications. He had been caught up to Paradise, and had seen and heard things which defied description, and which, even if they could have been described, were of such surpassing grandeur and sacredness that it would have been profanation to divulge them. Those rapturous apocalypses would no doubt prostrate the apostle in self-abasement at the time; but reflection on them afterwards might easily tend to feed a subtle tendency to self-importance, in that he had been the object of such dazzling Divine favours. Thus, he writes "lest I should be exalted above measure *through the abundance of the revelations. . . .*"

This is most striking. Those revelations were among the most wonderful of all the God-planned preparations of Paul for his great ministry. They were considered a necessary part of his equipment. Yet the very privileges which prepared him for special service were in themselves a danger and a source of temptation! So is it often with ourselves. Gifts, talents, capabilities, and other personal or social advantages entrusted to us, which others do not possess, and which are meant to fit us for service, and to fill us with humble gratitude to God, may be the very things which tempt us to vainglory. O how we need to watch against that shadowy monster, Pride! He has a velvet tread, and is often upon us ere we are aware of it. God give us the meek and lowly disposition of the Master! "In lowliness of mind let each esteem other better than themselves."

A third lesson here is that *times of great blessing are often followed by times of great trial.* What a contrast between being "caught up to Paradise," seeing the Lord face to face in all His celestial magnificence, the physical senses, for the time being, superseded, the body forgotten, and the spirit enlarged to receive visions of surpassing glory amid the angels and principalities of heavenly places—what a contrast, I say, between all that and being back in the body again, with a "thorn in the flesh," and a "messenger of Satan" to "buffet" him! We do not wonder that the apostle, stunned by this sudden Satanic reprisal, and stung with sensitive grief, should with a bleeding heart implore his Lord to remove this grave trial. Nor do we wonder that his sympathetic Lord should speak a direct word of reassurance to His suffering servant, "My grace is sufficient for thee; for My strength is made perfect in (thy) weakness."

This sudden alternation from the heights to the depths, while it was peculiar to Paul in its details, was by no means peculiar in its *nature.* Such sweeping transitions from the one extreme to the other are not uncommon, alas. We see them in the earth-life even of the Lord Jesus Himself. Stand at Jordan's brink; see the opened heaven, the swift-descending Dove, and hear the voice from the excellent glory. Splendid moment! Yes, but the next moment a black cloud quenches the sun, and the glory of that baptism gives place to the gloom of the wilderness and the grim ordeal of the Tempter's onslaught: "Immediately the Spirit driveth Him into the wilderness, and He was there . . . tempted of Satan." Climb the mountain height; stand with the privileged three, and behold the glorious sight of the transfigured Christ, with the glorified Moses and Elijah in attendance;

see that overhanging curtain of glory, and hear again the thrilling thunder of the voice Divine. Never-to-be-forgotten experience! Yet they have scarce recovered from the sublime surprise of the glory-capped mountain-top before they are face to face with a fuming demoniac at the mountain-foot. When we have been on the glory-capped summit with Christ, we must be prepared to meet Apollyon in some near-by valley! If we are not ready we shall be dazed with surprise, and our spiritual ascensions will be followed by withering reactions.

Still another lesson here is that *increased blessings bring increased testings*. Paul had been endowed with special privileges. Special revelations involved special temptations. Those who enjoy privileges denied to the many must expect testings escaped by the many. When God gives us unique blessings, Satan besets us with unique temptations. Increased privileges always come to us with increased responsibilities on their backs. Accessions of outward advantages such as wealth or social position are full of risks. Accessions of inward light and power are also beset with perilous snares. If our Shepherd has to use the goad sometimes, if some "thorn in the flesh" is permitted, let us beware lest rebellious complainings bring still further correction upon us!

Again, we see here that *there is a ministry in affliction*. There are some well-meaning but misguided brethren about us who, if they had lived in Paul's day, would have chided the apostle for lack of faith because he was not healed, or ridded, of his evil besetment. They would have asked, with eyebrows high in surprise, "Paul, why don't you claim your healing as one of your redemption rights?" What would Paul have replied, think you? I know to the very letter what he would have said. He would have said, as he still says in this passage, "For this thing I besought the Lord thrice, that it might depart from me; and He said unto me: My grace is sufficient for thee, for My strength is made perfect in weakness. Most gladly therefore will I rather glory in my infirmities that the power of Christ may rest upon me."

That is Paul's answer. Here is one of the seeming anomalies of Christian experience. The very man who by the power of the Name had re-limbed the lame and healed the incurable and even resuscitated the deceased could not himself be healed! The very champion who had wielded the power of Christ to cast out demons could not free himself from the buffetings of this "messenger of Satan"!

There is often indeed a gracious ministry in suffering. Before ever we think of "claiming" healing, we should ascertain whether it is an ordinary sickness, brought about by natural causes, or an "affliction"—some Divinely imposed measure of correction, with which we are dealing. James makes this distinction. "Is any sick among you? let him call for the elders of the church; and let them pray over him, anointing him with oil in the name of the Lord; and the prayer of faith shall save the sick and the Lord shall raise him up; and if he have committed sins, they shall be forgiven him." "Is any among you afflicted? let him pray" (Jas. v. 14, 15 and 13). Healing is not promised for "affliction." The only prescription is "pray." To be "claiming" deliverance from something which God Himself has purposively imposed or permitted is to be at cross purposes with the will of God! There was a wonderful ministry in Paul's suffering. If the "thorn" had been taken away from *him*, some of his writings would have been taken away from *us*. It was a thing which Christ Himself thought good for Paul to bear. All men have troubles in the flesh, for there is no perfect health, and no human body is free from ailments; but Paul's "thorn" was a super-addition to existing infirmities. Yet can we not see how this affliction, sanctified by the Spirit, was specially adapted to guard him at an exposed point? Being the object of a peculiar and virulent opposition, he was singularly liable to the temptation of over-asserting himself and his merits —and the more so, perhaps, because his enemies seemingly enjoyed jibing him about his defects in manner and appearance. Let it be settled in our minds that behind the afflictions which come to us there is always a wise and gracious purpose.

There is another striking disclosure in this passage, for we see here *Satanic agency in human suffering.* Paul himself clearly recognized that there was Satanic activity behind what had come to him. He says, "There was given to me a thorn in the flesh, *the messenger of Satan* to buffet me." The word translated "messenger" is really "angel"—an "*angel*" of Satan! Satan has his angels! There are harassing spirits as well as ministering spirits! It is not surprising that the arch-fiend should set apart one of his subordinate officers solely to concentrate on Paul, for the apostle was doing such damage to his dark kingdom. We may be quite sure, too, that this "angel of Satan" would have a bad time as well as Paul! When he reported to his captain he would have to report, "Cannot break through *there*!"

Years ago, two captured British generals were kept prisoners in a little room at the rear of the palace of Tippu Sultan, that old Mohammedan tyrant-king. One of the captured generals was Sir David Baird; and he, like his fellow prisoner, was kept chained to guards. When word was sent to his old mother in Scotland, the dour old lady, knowing her son, said: "Well, God have mercy on the poor chap that is chained to our Davy!" Perhaps the case is not altogether unparallel with that of Paul and the dark assailant from Satan. Shall we say "thank God!" or "alas!" that there is no need for such a concentrated attack of Satan upon some of ourselves? Perhaps we are not sufficiently damaging Satan's kingdom! It is well to realize, however, that there is indeed Satanic agency in not a little human suffering; and to realize this is the first step toward intelligently combating it.

Yet although there is Satanic agency here, we see also that *the Divine sovereignty is the ultimate reality*. Paul recognizes this as much as he detects the agency of Satan. He says: "There *was given* unto me a thorn in the flesh, an angel of Satan." This thing was "given." Ultimately it was from God. It was divinely permitted and overruled. Satan has rebelled against God's ruling; but he cannot escape God's *over*ruling; and even he is made to serve God's ends! The serpent is trodden to the dust, and God is sovereign. What comfort for buffeted saints is there in the Divine sovereignty! "All things work together for good to them that love God, to them who are the called *according to His purpose.*"

But see now *the severity of this Satanically inflicted suffering*. "There was given to me a *thorn* in the flesh." The Greek word translated "thorn" comes from a verb which means to impale or crucify. Paul's thorn was not the sort of thorn with which we prick a finger. It was a *stake* (A.S.V. margin) on which, so to speak, he was transfixed, even as his Lord was transfixed on the cross of Calvary; and as Paul was pinioned to this stake, an "angel of Satan" *buffeted* him, that is, dealt blow after blow upon him. Weymouth's translation brings all this out most forcefully.

Lest I should be over-elated there has been sent to me, like the agony of impalement, Satan's angel dealing blow after blow, lest I should be over-elated. Three times have I besought the Lord to rid me of him; but His reply has been "My grace suffices for you, for (My) power matures in weakness."

What depth of agony is here! Think, too, how long-drawn-out it was. It had been going on for fourteen years at the time when the apostle wrote these words. See how the chapter begins: "Fourteen years ago . . . caught up to Paradise . . . abundance of revelations . . . lest I should be exalted above measure . . . there was given me a thorn . . ." Fourteen years of long-drawn-out crucifixion and Satanic buffeting! What is more, at the time of writing there was seemingly no abatement! What is more still, it seemed as though the thing must go dragging on to the end of life! What an ordeal! "Who is sufficient for these things?" Paul shall tell us.

See here, finally, a magnificent demonstration of *victory through Christ*. "My strength is made perfect in (thy) weakness," says the Risen One to His suffering servant. The pronoun "My" does not come in some of the manuscripts, but the sense of the passage requires it as clearly as the glory of noonday requires the sun. To make the statement impersonal is to sap away the quintessence of it. It is "*My* strength"—the strength of *Jesus*, which is to find its opportunity in Paul's weakness. "*My strength*"—not so much that solitary might which belongs to Christ by original right as the Son of God, as, rather, that saving strength which He Himself acquired when in the days of His flesh He lived and laboured and suffered and struggled and bled to become our Saviour. *That* strength—the sympathetic Saviour's strength, which itself reached perfection through suffering, is infused into the heart and life of the believer. He who has victoriously undergone all our human experiences shares *His* victory with *us*. Christian experience does not run on the battery system—a being charged and then gradually running down, and then being recharged and running down again. It goes on the electric circuit principle—continuous current through continuous contact. Christ does not strengthen us by a periodic succession of miracles, but by a continuous communication of Himself to us through the Holy Spirit. Thus are we enabled to say: "I can do (or bear) all things through Christ who strengtheneth me." It is thus that the strength of Christ finds its opportunity in our weakness. When we are self-sufficient there is no scope for the imparted strength of Christ; but when some such agony as Paul's plunges us into the consciousness of utter destitution and we fling ourselves in helpless prostration at the feet of Christ, then, in our very extremity, Christ finds His opportunity. His strength then has its perfect work within us; and upon the ruins of our shattered self-sufficiency we rise to new life and victory in Christ! It was thus that Paul himself learned the secret of strength in weakness. It was thus that bewildering repulse was turned into riotous triumph, and the apostle pressed forward singing, "Most gladly therefore will I rather glory in my weaknesses, that the power of Christ may rest upon me. Therefore I take pleasure in weaknesses, in reproaches, in necessities, in persecutions, in distresses, for Christ's sake; for when I am weak, then am I strong."

When we are living the self-sufficient life, we are weakest where we are strongest, for there we are most unsuspectingly liable to surprise attack; but when we are living by the principle of sufficiency through the imparted strength of Christ, then we are strongest where we are weakest, for at our weakest point the strength of Christ has its most perfect opportunity. Edinburgh Castle has been captured only once in its history. The height and steepness of the great rock on which it is built were thought to make it quite impregnable on one side; and so no sentries were put there. In the mist of the early morning a party of attackers clambered up the rugged slopes, and surprised the garrison into surrender. The castle was taken at its strongest point. The same thing happened in 1759, when Wolfe and his men, under cover of night, climbed the Heights of Abraham on the north bank of the St. Lawrence, surprised the French at the unexpected point, and captured Quebec. The same thing has happened again and again in military history, and it happens, the world over, in individual human experience. Christian, mark well this double paradox of the spiritual life: **in ourselves we are weak even where we are strong; in Christ** we are strong even where we are weak. Self-sufficiency is *in*sufficiency. Christ-sufficiency is *all*-sufficiency.

"*My strength is made perfect in weakness.*" The words were spoken to Paul; and Paul has left them on record as part of a personal testimony; but do they really have meaning in the experience of Christ's people on earth to-day? The words have a triple significance. They express a *principle.* They describe a *process.* They convey a *promise.* Is the principle still valid? Is the process still operative? Is the promise still being fulfilled? Is this treble meaning of the text a demonstrable reality in present-day experience? In answer to that question, the following testimony is submitted, from a paper by the Rev. R. L. Lacey.

A Baptist minister writes: "When I was in Australia I kept hearing stories about a woman, a cripple, and I never believed them. I went to see her. I went to offer comfort, but before I had been in the room ten minutes I found it was I who was receiving instruction. When she was eighteen she was seized with a dread malady, and the doctor said that to save her life he must take off the foot. Both feet went. They followed the disease up the body; took off her legs to the knees, still following it up, and cut as far as the trunk. Then it broke out in her hands. The first arm went to the shoulder; and when I saw the lady, all that remained of her was a trunk. For fifteen years she had been there. I found the walls of the room covered with texts, all of them speaking of joy and peace and power; and I found that that woman, from her room, radiated such a power that scores, nay, literally hundreds of people had been converted or lifted by the letters she had written. She lay in her bed one day, and asked what she could do, a dismembered woman without a joint in her body. Then an inspiration came to her, and she got a friend, who was a carpenter, to come, and he fitted a pad to her shoulder, and then to that another, and a Swan fountain pen, and she began to write letters with it; and remember, when you write you write with your arm, but she has to write with the whole of her body. There may be clever calligraphists in this place, but I will undertake to say there is no woman in this congregation who could write a letter one half so beautiful from the point of view of calligraphy as she wrote in my presence, almost like copperplate. She had received fifteen hundred letters from people who had been brought to Christ through the letters she had written in that way from that room. I said to her: 'How do you do it?' She smiled, and replied: 'Well, you know, Jesus said that they who believed on Him, out of them should flow rivers of living water. I believed on Him, and that is all.'"

Wonderful? Here is the secret: "My strength is made perfect in weakness." Would those letters have been written and those fifteen hundred souls been won for Christ, if Christ had not found his opportunity in His servant's extremity?

We think of Annie Johnson Flint, the last and perhaps the sweetest of America's religious poets. She and her delicate sister were deprived of both parents early in life, and brought up with foster parents. Then, after schooling and an early going forth as bread-winner, Annie began to experience the first encroachments of arthritis. Her condition from that time steadily worsened until she was a completely crippled and helpless invalid, with even her foster parents now dead, and her sister too frail for the struggle to make ends meet. It would have been the easiest and most understandable thing in the world to lose heart and let faith go to pieces, even then; but there were severer testings to come. There were long, dragging years, not only of crippling physical twistedness, but of intense pain.

Mr. Philip E. Howard, president of the *Sunday School Times* Company, writes: "One day a visitor stepped from Miss Flint's sitting room into the sleeping room to secure a certain reprint of a poem for Miss Flint, who was seated in her wheeled chair. A glance at the bed in that room was revealing. Nine soft pillows were carefully arranged on the bed for use in protecting the exquisitely sensitive, pain-smitten body from the normal contact of the bedclothing, so distressing was it for her to recline in the hope of rest at night."

Can our Saviour's strength be "made perfect" even in such suffering and weakness as that? Well, it was this most sensitive sufferer who, out of her ordeal of protracted pain, sent out more "poem-pillows" for other suffering and discouraged hearts than perhaps any other poet of modern times. It was she who wrote—

God hath not promised
Skies ever blue,
Flower-strewn pathways
All our lives through;
God hath not promised
Sun without rain,
Joy without sorrow,
Peace without pain.

God hath not promised
Smooth roads and wide,
Swift, easy travel
Needing no guide;
God hath not promised
We shall not bear
Many a burden,
Many a care,

But God HATH promised
Strength for the day,
Rest amid labour,
Light for the way;
Grace for the trials,
Help from above,
Unfailing sympathy,
Undying love.

Troubled believer, have no doubt, Christ is true to His word. There faileth never one word of all His good promise to those who truly trust Him. Suddenly struck down with blindness when in the prime of life, George Matheson wrote the unforgettable lines—

My will is not my own
Till Thou hast made it Thine;
If it would reach the monarch's throne
It must its crown resign.
It only stands unbent
Amid the clashing strife,
When on Thy bosom it has leant,
And found in Thee its life.

Leaning on our Saviour's bosom, let us learn the source and all the *re*sources of our true life; and we shall find ourselves singing in quiet confidence, with Paul, "Most gladly therefore will I rather glory in my infirmities, that the power of Christ may rest upon me, . . . for when I am weak, then am I strong."

He never fails the soul that trusts in Him;
   He never fails.
Tho' disappointments come and hope burns dim,
   He never fails.
Tho' trials surge like stormy seas around,
Tho' testings fierce like ambushed foes abound,
Yet this my soul, with millions more has found,
   He never fails; He *never* fails.

He never fails the soul that trusts in Him;
   He never fails.
Tho' angry skies with thunder-clouds grow grim,
   He never fails.
Tho' icy blasts life's fairest flow'rs lay low,
Tho' earthly springs of joy all cease to flow,
Yet still 'tis true, with millions more I know,
   He never fails; He *never* fails.

He never fails the soul that trusts in Him;
   He never fails.
Tho' sorrow's cup should overflow the brim,
   He never fails.
Tho' oft the pilgrim way seems rough and long,
I yet shall stand amid yon white-robed throng,
And there I'll sing, with millions more, this song—
   He never fails; He *never* fails.

J. S. B.

MY PRESENCE

The presence of God's glory is in heaven; the presence of His power on earth; the presence of His justice in hell; and the presence of His grace with His people. If He deny us His powerful presence, we fall into nothing; if He deny us His gracious presence, we fall into sin; if He deny us His merciful presence we fall into hell. —JOHN MASON.

As the king of Sodom said unto Abraham, "Give me the persons, and take the goods to thyself," so say gracious souls, Give us more and more of the presence of God, and let the men of the world take the world and divide it amongst themselves. A soul that hath but tasted the sweetness of it (the Divine presence) cannot but long for more of it, as those that had tasted of the grapes of Canaan longed to be in Canaan. They that have experienced the sweetness of the Divine presence cannot be satisfied with a little of it, but in every prayer this is the language of their souls: Lord, more of Thy presence!—THOMAS BROOKS.

MY PRESENCE

"My presence shall go with thee, and I will give thee rest."
—Exod. xxxiii. 14.

I DO NOT know which are the more gracious and wonderful among the promises of the Bible, those addressed to *seekers* after God, or those addressed to the redeemed, who have *found* God in Christ. No pages in any other literature are lustred with such golden encouragements as we have here. The apostle Peter speaks of them as "exceeding great and precious promises"; and truly they are exceedingly great and precious— great both in number and nature, and precious both in the hope they inspire and in their solid reality.

Many of us, as we look back to the days when we first sought the Lord, can remember the promises which then meant to us more than ever we could tell. I well remember how I feasted my own eyes upon the almost unbelievable graciousness of those two texts, "Him that cometh unto Me I will in no wise cast out," and "He that believeth on the Son hath everlasting life." As for the years since that happy day which "fixed our choice," we can only say that the promises of our faithful God have become more and more precious to us as we have again and again tried and proved them.

Now there is one class of promises which has always had a specially tender appeal to the Lord's people. It is that large group in which we have *the assurance of the Divine presence with us.* If there is one thing more than another which the true servants of God have always longed to be quite sure about, it is this very thing, the Divine presence; and God has graciously responded in the many assurances given to us in His word.

How wonderful are these promises of the Divine presence! They constitute one of the most comforting and edifying studies in the Bible. The merest glance at some of them is enough to fill the desponding heart with fresh courage and gladness. Still more, when we ponder them carefully, examining their terms and considering the circumstances in which they were given, do we discover indeed the " exceeding great " riches which we possess in them. As a specimen, let us take the promise given to Moses: " My presence shall go with thee, and I will give thee rest." This promise in particular commends itself because it lays even added stress upon the fact of the Divine presence, in that precious pronoun "My"—"*My* presence shall go with thee, and I will give thee rest."

The promise is a benediction in itself: but it is when we take it with its context that its fuller graciousness and glory break upon us. However beautiful a jewel may be in itself, its beauty is enhanced by an appropriate setting. However lovely a full-blown rose may be in isolation, it has its loveliest look and fullest fragrance when it blooms in its native bower. So is it with this promise. We shall therefore consider it in a threefold way:

The *setting* of it—in the life of Moses;
The *wording* of it—as it came from God;
The *proving* of it—in our own experience.

First, then, we will consider the SETTING of this promise in the life of Moses. It was spoken to Moses in connection with one of the most deplorable incidents in the wilderness journeyings of Israel. God had raised up a deliverer to bring the people out from the grovelling bondage of Egypt into national freedom and blessing in Canaan. He had accomplished their emancipation with mighty hand and outstretched arm. He had demonstrated his presence with them by miraculous interventions, preserving, protecting, providing, in wonderful ways. Yet now, while Moses is in the mount, receiving the commandments, and the instructions regarding the Tabernacle, the people have " turned aside quickly " to idolatry, and are dancing, naked, before the golden calf! Moses returns to the camp, and sees the idol-worship in progress. The tables of the law drop from his trembling hands. He seizes the wretched image, burns it in the fire, and then grinds it to powder. But if the first sight of Israel's idolatrous obscenity kindles the anger of Moses, the thought of it afterwards dazes him with grief. A broken-hearted man, he sinks down before God, and sobs out the pitiful prayer:

"Oh, this people have sinned a great sin, and have made them gods of gold. Yet now, if Thou wilt forgive their sin—; and if not, blot me, I pray thee, out of Thy book which Thou hast written."

The Divine answer is:

"Whosoever hath sinned against Me, him will I blot out of My book. Therefore now go, lead the people unto the place of which I have spoken unto thee: behold Mine angel shall go before thee: nevertheless in the day when I visit, I will visit their sin upon them. Depart and go up hence, thou and the people which thou hast brought up out of the land of Egypt, unto the land which I sware unto Abraham, to Isaac, and to Jacob, saying: Unto thy seed will I give it. And I will send an angel before thee, and I will drive out the Canaanite, the Amorite, and the Hittite, and the Perizzite, the Hivite, and the Jebuzite: unto a land flowing with milk and honey: for I will not go up in the midst of thee (for thou art a stiffnecked people) lest I consume thee in the way."

A gracious answer indeed! Yet to a man like Moses, heart-broken, disillusioned, apprehensive about the future, and yearning more than ever for the assurance of the Divine companionship, such an answer was an answer and yet *no* answer. What consolation was there in the words, "I will send an angel before thee"? It was not angels but the presence of God Himself for which Moses was pleading. What was it that the Canaanites should be dispossessed, and Israel gain the "land flowing with milk and honey," if God himself were not with the people? God's blessings without Himself are no blessings at all to the God-hungry heart. One of the old-time kings of England, becoming displeased with the City Fathers, threatened to remove the royal court from London to some other place. The Mayor replied: "As long as he leaves the River Thames we will do very well." It is by no means thus with the saint and his God. All the blessings of Canaan are no compensation for the absence of the Divine companionship. This is how God's true servants have ever felt. This is how Moses felt. "If *Thy* presence go not with me, carry us not up hence," he says: and it was in loving kindness toward his heart-stricken servant that God gave this further assurance, "MY PRESENCE shall go with thee."

Thus we see, in the first place, that this promise was spoken to a *disappointed* man, a man into whose life there had suddenly come a disheartening disillusionment. The people on whom such high hopes were set had proved faithless! The tables of the law lay in fragments below the mount! The wrath of God burned against the stiff-necked idolaters! Poor Moses! His disappointment must have been great beyond our knowing. It was to *this* man, and at *this* time, that the comforting word was given, "My presence shall go with thee, and I will give thee rest."

Am I speaking even now to some disappointed Christian man or woman? You started out with godly intentions and high hopes, but experience has brought disillusionment, denial, unexpected turns of frustration, and now you are disappointed with life? There is an incurable, dull ache in your heart about the way things have transpired? Friend, this promise is specially for *you*!—"My presence shall go with thee, and I will give thee rest." God delights to dwell with the disappointed, that their sense of disappointment may be swallowed up in the super-abounding compensation of His heart-satisfying and rest-bringing sympathy and friendship. Disconsolate heart, seek the face of a sympathetic heavenly Father. Ask the fulfilling of His promise. He is with you and wanting to become so real to you that disappointment shall be transformed into triumph by His realized presence.

When the Rev. Henry F. Lyte found there was no hope of his recovery from consumption, he went into his study, looked death straight in the face, and sat down to write the brave and beautiful words,

> " I fear no foe with Thee at hand to bless;
> Ills have no weight, and tears no bitterness;
> Where is death's sting? Where grave thy victory?
> I triumph still, if THOU abide with me."

Ah, yes, we may "triumph still," for God has said, "My presence *shall* go with thee, and I will give thee rest."

Again, this promise was spoken to a *discouraged* man, a man whose great work for God seemed to be falling to pieces. How deeply discouraged must Moses have been! Not only have the people proved utterly undependable and perverted, and three thousand Israelites fallen by the swords of their own brothers, and the "tabernacle" been removed from the corrupted camp, but God Himself has indicated the withdrawal of His personal presence from the people. True, God has said that an angel shall lead the host, but an angel's presence without God himself means mere guidance without fellowship. Discouraged and dispirited, Moses plaintively expostulates: "See, Thou sayest unto me, Bring up this people; and Thou hast not let me know whom Thou wilt send with me (if an angel, which?). Yet Thou hast said, I know thee by name, and thou hast also found grace in My sight. Now therefore, I pray Thee, if I have found grace in Thy sight, show me now Thy way, that I may know Thee, that I may find grace in Thy sight; and consider that this is *Thy* people."

And am I even now speaking to some discouraged Christian? Friend, tell me, why those falling tears? You have been very jealous for the honour of the Lord, and it has seemed to occasion nothing but misunderstanding? You have been faithfully witnessing for your Saviour, yet you have seen no souls coming out for Him? You have been earnestly seeking to win those Sunday School scholars, yet they seem unresponsive, and you have become dismayed? You have been seeking for fuller spiritual life and victory, but somehow it has not come, and a recoil of depression has taken you? Ah, discouraged child of God, this promise is specially for you, " My presence shall go with thee, and I will give thee rest." Are you looking to God to fulfil this promise to you, or are you doubting his tenderness and faithfulness? Are you taking time—are you *making* time— to seek God's face as Moses did? He loves you dearly, He bought you for Himself at the infinite cost of Calvary. He is really with you, and He wants to make His presence a "living, bright reality" in your experience. In the realizing of His presence lies the secret of unfailing courage.

Years ago, the Rev. Robert Bruce, a saintly Scottish minister, attracted many people to his church. On one occasion an earl drove a good distance to one of the services, and, getting impatient for the service to commence, he asked the beadle when the minister would appear. The officer went to the vestry door, but hearing conversation within, he refrained from knocking, and then returned to the earl, saying, "He wunna come to-day, yer lordship, for I heerd him say to Someone that he canna gae withoot Him; and though he keepit on asking, I didna hear the Other answer him at a'!" Thank God, we have the assurance that the "Other" One is *always* with us, sharing all our experiences, saving us from discouragement, giving our hearts sweet rest. "My presence shall go with thee, and I will give thee rest."

Once again, we note that this promise was spoken to a very *diffident* man, a man bending beneath the weight of a great responsibility, feeling that his burden was more than he could bear, and apprehensive about the future. Did ever a man carry a heavier burden than Moses? Is it surprising that above all else he longed for the assurance of the Divine presence with him? Going with the sense of responsibility there would likely enough be a sense of loneliness. When God calls a man out for special leadership and responsibility, or for some deeper experience of Himself, it always means a certain loneliness. If we obey "the heavenly vision" our very obedience means that we must tread a path where God wants us alone, and where others cannot accompany us. Loneliness has been a dread ordeal with many great servants of God, and has made them long for the compensating consciousness of the Lord's own presence with them.

And has God failed them? To all those who bear heavy burdens, and to all who are lonely because of their attachment to the Lord Jesus, this promise comes with its heavenly cheer, "My presence shall go with thee, and I will give thee rest."

> Yea I am with thee when there falls no shadow
>   Across the golden glory of the day,
> And I am with thee when the storm-clouds gather,
>   Dimming the brightness of the onward way;
> In days of loss, and loneliness and sorrow,
>   Of care and weariness and fretting pain,
> In days of weakness and of deep depression,
>   Of futile effort when thy life seems vain;
> When youth has fled, and Death has put far from thee
>   Lover and Friend who made the journey sweet,
> When Age has come with slowly failing powers,
>   And the dark valley waits thy faltering feet;
> When courage fails thee for the unknown future;
>   And the heart sinks beneath its weight of fears;
> Still I am with thee—Strength and Rest and Comfort,
>   Thy Counsellor through all Earth's changing years.
> Whatever goes, whatever stays,
>   My presence shall be with thee all the days.

Look now at the WORDING of the promise, as it comes to us from the lips of God. We may use the anthropomorphism "the lips of God," without any hesitation, because the promise is recorded as having been spoken directly to Moses by God Himself: "*He said:* My presence shall go with thee, and I will give thee rest."

The first word in the promise is that precious pronoun "*My*"; and it is this pronoun which has the emphasis here. God's promise to send an angel far from satisfied Moses. He now at length tenderly yields to His servant's moving entreaty, and says: "*My* presence shall go with thee." The Septuagint Version, recognizing the emphasis on the pronoun here, translates it "I Myself will go with thee." That priceless "My" pledges to us the side-by-side, step-by-step, heart-to-heart fellowship of *God Himself* through all our way. Oh how much this means to the spiritual mind! We can bear the loss of all things so long as we do not lose the presence of Him Whom our soul loveth. His absence is our midnight; His smile our noontide brightness.

> Take from me anything Thou wilt,
>   But go not *Thou* away;
> And let the storm that does Thy will
>   Deal with me as it may.

Look at the next word in the promise. "My *presence* shall go with thee." This meant far more than infallible superintendence from a distant heaven. It meant the close companionship of One who was enough to meet all Moses' need for guidance and sustenance and strength. An unchanging, undeparting Friend should company with him through all the wilderness journeyings, a wonderful Friend who would sit with him in the tent, stand with him in the council, and go forth with him on the field of battle. All sense of loneliness should be lost in the abiding presence of One who was at the same time absolutely almighty and infinitely sympathetic.

Translated literally, the word reads: "My *face* shall go with thee." How richly expressive is this! It bespeaks *intimacy* of fellowship. In some wonderful way there was to be face-to-face communion. What inspiration this must have meant for Moses! What inspiration it brings to ourselves!—for "*all* the promises of God" are "yea and amen" unto *us*, in Christ. This promise which was originally given to Moses is now part of *our* property. The face of God to *us* is the face of Jesus. "He that hath seen Me hath seen the Father," says our Lord Jesus; and in a spiritual sense *we* have seen Jesus, and in Him have seen the Father. Yea, more, we *do* see Jesus, and we *do* see the Father, all the time. That dear and wonderful face is always with us, and present to the eye of our faith. The natural man declares this to be mere imagination, but he knows not whereof he affirms, being blinded by the spiritual darkness in which he himself is existing. If it *is* just imagination, then it is the most sanctifying delusion which ever captured the imaginative faculties of the human mind. The real truth, however, is that it is no mere imagination at all. It is the natural man himself who is deceived. "The natural man receiveth not the things of the Spirit of God, neither can he know them because they are spiritually discerned." "My *face* shall go with thee." The boundless God becomes our bosom Friend! Well may the true Christian sing,

> Oh, the pure delight of a single hour
>   Which before Thy throne I spend,
> When I kneel in prayer, and with Thee, my *God*,
>   I commune *as friend with friend*!

"My *face* shall go with thee." Besides suggesting close fellowship, this expression speaks of *radiance*. "My face"— this was the beautiful antidote to Moses' gloomy anxiety. There can be no darkness in that life where regular communion with God keeps the soul bathed in the glory-light of the Divine smile. What the ever-present radiance of God's face meant to Moses we may gather from the fact that when, later, the priests of Israel were given a form of benediction with which to pronounce blessing upon the people, the words which Moses handed on to them were,

"The Lord bless thee and keep thee: The Lord make HIS FACE SHINE upon thee and be gracious unto thee. The Lord lift up HIS COUNTENANCE upon thee, *and give thee peace*."—Num. vi. 24, 26.

This very word "shine" is used of the face of Jesus. "God hath *shined* into our hearts, to give the light of the knowledge

of the glory of God in the face of Jesus Christ" (2 Cor. iv. 6).
Can we ever tell all that it means to us to go through our days
with that dear face imaged in our hearts, making our lives
like a sunlit Emmaus walk?

"My *face* shall go with thee." Here, too, is the thought of
the Divine *approval and goodwill* toward us. The face is that
which expresses the heart. Disapproval is often indicated by
the turning away of the face. God condescendingly accom-
modates Himself to our human ways of speaking and doing,
in this anthropomorphism, "My face shall go with thee," thus
indicating His gracious favour. "The face of the Lord is against
them that do evil," says the psalmist; and again "God be
merciful unto us, and bless us, and cause His face to shine
upon us." The Divine favour is ever beaming upon the true
believer from the face of Jesus Christ. Having "chosen us in
Him before the foundation of the world, "God has "blessed us
with all spiritual blessings in heavenly places in Christ," until,
in the coming Consummation, He unfolds to us, through the
eternal ages, the "exceeding riches of His grace in His kindness
toward us through Christ Jesus."

Look at the *certainty* of the promise. It says "My presence
shall go with thee." The Divine assurances are never enfeebled
by any suggestion of falteringness. They are all "yea and
amen," doubly sure. Dear Christian, when God says "My
presence shall go with thee" He means that without any
peradventure He will be with each of us right through to the
end. If God be with us even death is disarmed of all dread.
Hear again John Wesley's death-bed exultation, "The best of
all is GOD IS WITH US!"

> The soul that on Jesus has leaned for repose,
> He will not, He will not desert to its foes;
> That soul, though all hell should endeavour to shake,
> He'll never, no *never*, no NEVER forsake!

How comforting is the second clause of the promise!—"*I will
give thee rest.*" Bishop Handley Moule observes: "There are
two possible sorts of rest. One is rest *after* toil, the lying down
of the weary, at the end of the march, on the morrow of the
battle, on the summit of the hill. The other is rest *in* toil,
the internal and deep repose and liberty of a spirit which has

found a hidden refuge and retreat, where feeling is calm and disengaged, while the march, the battle, the climb, are still in full course." It was this latter kind of rest which was promised in God's word to Moses; not rest *after*, but rest *in*. This is the kind of rest that *we* need. What restlessness there is to-day! What hurry and strain! What unsettledness and tension! How wearying it can be both nervously and spiritually! How easily can the Christian get worn down and become nervous, anxious, agitated, fainthearted! How we need the soothing inward quiet which God here promises! There is nothing better for the nervous system than the peace of God in the heart.

"*I will give thee rest.*" The "rest" grows out of the "presence." The steadying consciousness of God's presence and favour gives to the heart a rest which nothing else can ever give. It gives rest from *doubts*, for when God is real doubt dies. It gives rest from *fear*, for if God be for us who can be against us? It gives rest from *anxiety*, for if God walks with us nothing can really harm us. It gives rest from misgiving about the future, for all things must work together for our good.

"*I will give thee rest.*" Why, these are the very words that fell from the lips of Jesus: "Come unto Me all ye that labour and are heavy laden, and *I will give you rest.*" Ah, it is in Jesus that God fulfils His promised rest to us. It is in the realized presence of the risen Lord that the Christian finds a repose of heart which the world can neither give nor take away.

And now consider the PROVING of this gracious promise in our own experience. Did not God make good His word to Moses? Has He not honoured it in the lives of millions more? Will He not then fulfil it to ourselves? "O thou of little faith, wherefore didst thou doubt?" No word of His can fall to the ground.

God never denies to His people that which is necessary for them; and He *knows*, as truly as we ourselves *feel*, the indispensability of His presence with us. In our present life on earth we are incessantly subject to temptation and testing. As the members of Adam's race there is that within us which makes us the all-too-easy prey of sin. Temptations lie everywhere around us in most innocent guise. In the nature of things, and as we ourselves are at present, anything can become a temptation and a snare. However clever we may be in other ways, by nature we are all easily deceived in spiritual things, in the things of the soul, the things that most really matter, the things that determine our eternal destiny.

But besides what we may call negative temptations, that is, those temptations which arise through the wrong reaction of our own natures to things which are innocent enough in themselves, there are solicitations positively forced upon us every hour we live, by virile evil influences. Satan, that cunning strategist with six millenniums of practice in the cruel art of tricking souls into sin, is more than our match; and, besides this, it is a matter of Scripture revelation that leagues of spiritual agencies are in confederacy with the arch-enemy, bent on our undoing.

How we need the protection of God's own presence! Prosperity can be to us "the destruction that wasteth at noonday." Adversity can be to us "the pestilence that walketh in darkness." Swift temptation comes as "the arrow that flieth by day." Secret enticement comes as "the terror by night." The "snare of the fowler" is ever ready to entangle us; and the "noisome pestilence" is ever ready to seize upon us. Every hour we need the protecting presence of our God and Saviour.

I need Thy presence every passing hour;
What but Thy grace can foil the tempter's power?
Who like Thyself my guide and stay can be?
Through cloud and sunshine, O abide with me.

Thank God, the Divine presence with us is as great a reality as it is a necessity. How many millions of departed saints would be glad to rise up and give testimony to this fact! Nor is the Lord's presence less real to-day among those who are in truth His own. Who shall put into words all that the Divine presence has meant to the people of Christ through the years, and still means to-day? Even when we are not sensitive to it He is with us (and it is all too true that many of us know little enough about the experiential realization of our Lord's company); but He would have His presence to be "a living, bright reality" to us in our daily life; and so it may be if we walk with Him as Enoch did, as Moses and Daniel did, and as many another has done.

What a difference it makes to our life when we discover that our dear Lord is really with us! What a transforming effect Jacob's discovery of the Divine presence had upon him! When he fled from Isaac's tents he thought he had left his father's God behind. He did not yet know the Lord Jehovah in a true way. Jacob's exclamation was one of astonishment, "Surely the Lord is in this place, and I knew it not." It was a life-transforming discovery, as we see from the vow he there uttered.

There was a Hebrew prophet once, who thought to sail beyond the reach of "the presence of the Lord." Had he only read certain verses from the Pentateuch, for his Scripture reading that morning, or a few verses from Psalm cxxxix, he would never have paid his fare! Later, he was grateful to find that even his strange submarine voyage could not shut him off from God! What a comfort was the presence of the Lord to Paul as he took his trial before Nero!—"At my first answer (defence) no man stood with me, but all men forsook me: I pray God that it may not be laid to their charge. Notwithstanding, the Lord stood with me, and strengthened me."

And how real has the Lord's presence been to multitudes of others! One could fill pages, or rather whole books, with quotations from testimonies borne by His people to this effect. The danger is that in picking out examples here and there we should give the impression that such examples are unusual, or such as may only be experienced by a certain few of the Lord's flock. No, God is not a respecter of persons. The vivid and supporting consciousness of His presence may be known by the humblest among us. Hear what He saith: "I dwell in the high and holy place; with him also that is of a contrite and humble spirit." There is no good reason why the realization of the Divine presence should not be a constant and cloudless experience with us. A book which I never read without being greatly impressed is *Mile-stone Papers*, by the late Rev. Daniel Steele, D.D., and from the latter part of this book, where the author gives ten priceless papers which he calls "Experimental Essays," we give the following composite quotation relating to his realization of the Divine presence and indwelling. Looking back over the years of his joyous experience, he writes as here given.

"During these cloudless, blissful years—dare I write it—my soul and body have been the abode of the indwelling Christ, *consciously* 'the habitation of God through the Spirit'. Almost every week, and sometimes every day, the pressure of His great love comes down upon my heart, an almost insupportable plethora of joy. I once walked much amid the shadows, having a streak of sunshine sandwiched with streaks of twilight, with occasionally darkness that could be felt. How changed is all this now! Christ is not a capricious dweller in the temple of my heart, present to-day and absent to-morrow. *He abides.* My joy in Christ has waxed, not waned, during these ten blissful years. As if to prove that this is not mere animal feeling, the result of favourable bodily conditions and an agreeable environment, God has been pleased to put forth His hand and touch my body, taking away my strength, while He has given to me no exemption from what men call troubles, crosses, and disappointments; yet none of these things moves me. The storms which rudely sweep the earth's surface produce not even a ripple on the face of the water in the deep well."

The late Rev. Asa Mahan, D.D., one-time principal of Oberlin Theological College, leaves the following testimony, among many other valuable papers.

"The manner in which Christ first 'manifested Himself' to me will, I doubt not, be held in remembrance to eternity. I had risen from my knees in my study: the veil was lifted, and Christ, not as an object of physical, but exclusively mental and spiritual vision, was immediately before me. With open face I beheld 'the light of His countenance' lifted upon me. Then I realised, as I had never done before, not only that He had 'given Himself' for me, but that 'He loved me,' and was present to me, to show me the beauty of my Lord, and, as my eternal Friend and Portion, to abide in me for ever. All I could say was that my joy was full. The 'brightness of that rising' has never passed away, but is in the soul as an everlasting and ever-growing light. I read my inner life now in the words of the promise of God through His inspired prophet: 'The sun shall be no more thy light by day; neither for brightness shall the moon give light unto thee: but the Lord shall be unto thee an everlasting light, and thy God thy glory. Thy sun shall no more go down, neither shall thy moon withdraw itself; for the Lord shall be thine everlasting light, and the days of thy mourning shall be ended'."

We think of "Brother Lawrence," the seventeenth-century kitchen-servant, and his wonderful experience of the presence of God. We find him saying—

"The time of business does not with me differ from the time of prayer; and in the noise and clutter of my kitchen, while several persons are at the same time calling for different things, I possess God in as great tranquillity as if I were on my knees. . . . I make it my business only to persevere in His holy presence, wherein I keep myself by a simple attention, and an habitual, silent, and secret conversation of the soul with God, which often causes in me joys and raptures inwardly, and sometimes also outwardly, so great that I am forced to use means to moderate them, and prevent their appearance to others. . . . There is not in the world a kind of life more sweet and delightful than that of a continual conversation with God. Those only can comprehend it who practise and experience it; yet I do not advise you to do it from that motive; it is not pleasure which we ought to seek in this exercise; but let us do it from a principle of love, and because God would have us."

And what more shall we say?—for the time would fail us to tell of Thomas à Kempis, Madame Guyon, Hester Ann Rogers, William Carvosso, and a host of the early Methodists, and a bigger host still, from all denominations and times, who give similarly glad testimony to the reality of the Divine presence. Long ago, the famous Cæsar cheered up his drooping mariners by reminding them of his presence; but what was Cæsar's presence compared with this delectable heavenly companionship which the saints have enjoyed?

Dear Christian, canst thou not believe it?—this wondrous consciousness of thy Lord's continual presence is meant for *thee*. It is in no sense the exclusive portion of a privileged class. God does not deal with us in that way. Nor is it only possible to those whose circumstances allow hours of protracted retirement each day. True prayer is a bigger thing than can be confined to forms and times and places—though this by no means belittles the importance of our having regular and set times for prayer each day. Well does God know that most of us must give hours daily to other things; yet none the less He is with us, and we may develop such an uninterrupted consciousness of His presence as shall transfigure all our daily work, making life's dullest places bloom and smile. Moses, Joseph, Daniel, were all "men of affairs," having their hands full of what we call "non-religious" matters; yet how vivid was the nearness of God to them! The same could be said of a host whose names are not so familiar to us. Do some of us feel ourselves too small for God to think specially upon *us*? It is an enemy who hath suggested this. If God foreknew us, and loved us before we drew our first breath, and predestinated us unto the adoption of children, in Christ, will He fail to think upon us during our sojourn here? Will He whose watchful eye loses not sight of the falling sparrow turn His eye away from His own children? Will He who paints the wayside flower, as well as lights the evening star, be unmindful of those whom He has redeemed with the precious blood of Christ? However mean our earthly circumstances may be, we are "heirs of God, and joint-heirs with Christ"; and shall God forget His very elect?

> Among so many, can He care?
> Can special love be everywhere?
> A myriad homes, a myriad ways,—
> And God's eye over every place?—
> I asked. My soul bethought of this,—
> In just that very place of His
> Where God hath put and keepeth you,
> God hath no other thing to do!

O believer, dear to the great Father, made unspeakably precious to Him by the redemption-price paid on Calvary, made sacred to Him by the indwelling of the Holy Spirit, think over this great truth, that God would hold fellowship with thee every hour of the day. If we are conscientious and resolute to maintain some time or times of private prayer, and thoughtful Bible meditation, each day, and are willing to put from us vain ways and questionable practices, determining to love God with all our heart and mind and soul, and strength, we may "practise the presence of God," as Brother Lawrence did, and develop such a radiant realization of His fellowship with us as shall keep us always "rejoicing with joy unspeakable and full of glory." Thus will our pathway be illumined with a Divine light which will burn ever more brightly unto the perfect day of heaven.

MY PEACE

O blessed life!—the heart at rest,
When all without tumultuous seems,
That trusts a higher will, and deems
That higher will, not mine, the best.

O blessed life!—heart, mind, and soul
From self-born aims and wishes free;
In all—at one with Deity,
And loyal to the Lord's control.

O life, how blessed, how divine!
High life, the earnest of a higher!
Saviour fulfil my deep desire,
And let this blessed life be mine.

W. T. Matson.

MY PEACE

"Peace I leave with you: My peace I give unto you."—
John xiv. 27.

WHAT SHOULD we do without these later chapters of John?
How sublimely they unveil the heart of Jesus! What illumina-
tion they flash upon the thought processes of that matchless
mind in the hours leading up to the Cross! In these chapters
we are treading sacred soil. A voice Divine speaks from them
to the reverent reader as clearly as that which called to Moses
from the flaming bush of Horeb—"Put off thy shoes from off
thy feet, for the place whereon thou standest is holy ground."

In reading thoughtfully through these chapters we cannot fail
to be most deeply impressed by two facts which stand out above
all others in connection with Jesus Himself: first, that He
plainly knew of His approaching suffering; and secondly, that
He possessed perfect *peace*. We are struck with a kind of awed
surprise as, on the eve of His supreme ordeal, we see His
majestic movements, His complete composure, His calm
confidence, and as we hear Him quietly uttering to His apprehensive disciples the profoundest pronouncements and most
comforting truths of all His ministry.

In speaking about our Lord's peace, however, we need to have
clear views as to what peace really is. There are wrong ideas
about peace which lead men and women into delusion and
disappointment.

Peace is not merely *impassivity*, a negative quality, a condition of mind in which we remain completely unaffected by the
happenings and circumstances around us. There are those who
make a mistake here. They tell themselves that if they had real
peace they would never be roused into any concern or strong
emotion about the things outside them. Peace, they think, is a
passive condition in which one is quite insensible to the troublous
scenes of life. What does *anything* really matter? Why in the

least worry? Peace is quiescent unconcern, complete unrespon-
siveness; in a word, *absence of feeling.*

Well, that is not the true meaning of peace at all. We go into
a hospital ward and see a man who lies dying. There is no pain,
however, and no struggling; the man lies in a state of coma;
and we say, "How peaceful!" Yet is this real peace? Far from
it! It is the stupor of drugged faculties, the unintelligent void
of unconsciousness, the morbid insensibility of disease. No, this
is not peace. Many a godless man brags that he has no worry
about his sins. Does this mean that he has peace? No: it simply
shows that in a spiritual sense he is a *corpse.* We must not
confuse peace with apathy. Peace is not simply the absence of
disturbance; it is rather the presence of *an assurance* in the heart
which brings rest about everything else.

It is thus quite possible to have peace filling the mind and yet
to feel tremendously concerned about things outside. How
many of us there are who have found wonderful peace in Jesus,
and who are nevertheless much concerned about friends and
relatives who have not yet come to the Saviour! Yet there is
no incongruity in these two states simultaneously existing
within us. We know that our peace floweth as a river; yet we
could weep our eyes out for the salvation of our dear ones.

In the Lord Jesus Himself we see strong emotion blending in
perfect concord with His sublimely wonderful peace. Take two
of His utterances recorded in these later chapters of John. "Now
is My soul troubled; and what shall I say?" (xii. 27). "He was
troubled in spirit, and testified, and said: Verily, verily I say
unto you that one of you shall betray Me" (xiii. 21). The Lord
Jesus could be moved with compassionate concern for the
multitudes. He could sigh over the sufferings of the afflicted.
He could weep at the grave of Lazarus. He could marvel at
men's unbelief. He could thunder forth His anger at the
hypocrisy of the Scribes and Pharisees. He could be "troubled"
in prospect of His agony. He could suffer as no other. Yet this
is the One Who none the less gives to us the most wonderful
picture of peace we could ever find or desire, and who says to us:
"Peace I leave with you; My peace I give unto you; not as the
world giveth give I unto you. Let not your heart be troubled,
neither let it be afraid."

Let us clearly realize, then, that peace is not mere apathy or impassivity. Nor is it any stoic *suppression* of one's natural feelings, the artificial deadening of one's human sensibilities. Nor is peace mere *placidity*, the glassy smoothness on a sheet of still water. It has to do with the depths, not just the surface. Many a man contrives a placid exterior while his bosom inwardly bleeds with civil war. Nor is peace to be confused with the happy-go-lucky bravado of the God-forgetting worldling as he unconcernedly plunges into his pleasures. That insensibility to eternal realities which the world's follies engender is superficial, deceptive, and utterly false. Far better have storms of fear than such a calm as that—for terrible is the inevitable awakening which eventually comes!

Fundamentally, peace is a matter not of our emotions but of our *convictions*. In these days *opinions* have taken the place of convictions; that is why there is so little peace and so much restlessness. A man holds his own opinions, and changes them as he will; but a man's convictions hold *him*. A man will *argue* for his opinions; he will *die* for his convictions. As Sir Robert Anderson said, "Opinions are our own and should not be too firmly held. Truth is Divine, and is worth living and dying for." The martyrs did not die for their opinions; they died for their convictions. No man ever died for his opinions if he could help it; but men and women have gladly suffered diabolical torture and agonizing deaths for their unshakable belief in Divine truth. They held that truth to the spirit is more than life to the body; and they died in *peace*. How different with the many to-day! Like the wiseacres of ancient Athens, ever learning yet never able to come to a knowledge of the truth, numberless folks nowadays are always under the spell of the new book they have just read, or the latest idea put forward in the name of science or culture. These evanescent spells, one after another, spell restlessness!

Peace, we repeat, is fundamentally a matter of our convictions. It has to do with those beliefs which so grip us that they have become part of us; those truths of which we have an unshakable inward assurance; those things of the soul which are so precious and vital to us that we would sooner die than lose them. We sometimes hear it said: "Oh, that man holds his convictions lightly." Wrong! No man holds his convictions lightly. It is his opinions which he holds lightly. A man will hold opinions on the slenderest evidence. If he *wants* to think a certain way, he will take any bit of evidence for it at twice its worth. Not so our convictions, the things that are vital to us; they are the most intelligent things about us. If we really believe a thing "in dead earnest" *we know why.*

Convictions are thus seen to be built up on knowledge, belief, and assurance; and it is from these certainties of the soul that true peace comes. True peace is that restfulness which settles on the heart from an unshakable inward assurance concerning the vital issues of life. When we are *really gripped* by the intelligent assurance that all is working out for good, we have peace.

It is *this* which explains the wonderful peace of the Lord Jesus. His peace was the inward rest which came from His perfect knowledge and assurance. If we turn again to those later chapters of John we shall be profoundly impressed by the tremendous affirmations which Christ uttered concerning Himself, revealing His perfection of knowledge, and His omniscient assurance concerning ultimate issues.

Human hearts have always longed for knowledge and certainty about four greatly problematical and supremely important subjects, namely, the Divine, the Beyond, the Future, the Present. Now see the perfection of knowledge and assurance which the Lord Jesus displays respecting all four.

Observe His tremendous affirmations concerning Himself and His unique intimacy with the *Divine.*

"No man cometh unto the Father but by Me."—xiv. 6.
"I am in the Father, and the Father in Me."—xiv. 10.
"The Father that dwelleth in Me doeth the works."—xiv. 10.
"He that loveth Me shall be loved of My Father."—xiv. 21.
"I am the true Vine, and My Father is the Husbandman."—xv. 1.
"The Father hath loved Me."—xv. 9.
"He that hateth Me hateth my Father."—xv. 23.
"All things that the Father hath are Mine."—xvi. 15.

See our Lord's perfect knowledge of the *Beyond* expressing itself in such words as, "In My Father's house are many mansions; I go to prepare a place for you." Our Lord knew whence He was, and why He had come, and whither He was now returning. "I came out from the Father, and am come into the world: again I leave the world, and go to the Father."

See how, with the confidence of intimacy, He stresses the fact
five times over that He is going to the Father:—

"*I go unto the Father.*"—xiv. 12, xiv. 28, xvi. 10, xvi. 16, xvi. 28.

Observe, further, our Lord's calm assurance about the *Future*.

"I will come again, and receive you unto Myself, that where I am,
there ye may be also."—xiv. 3.

"The Father shall give you another Comforter that He may
abide with you for ever."—xiv. 16.

"I have told you before it come to pass, that when it is come to
pass ye may believe."—xiv. 29.

"A little while and ye shall not see Me; and again a little while
and ye shall see Me."—xvi. 16.

"They shall put you out of the synagogues (etc.) . . . . These
things have I told you that when the time shall come ye may
remember that I told you of them."—xvi. 2-4.

Yet again, see our Lord's perfect assurance about the *Present*.
As He speaks He knows that in the deepest sense of the word all
is well. Is He to be given into the hands of wicked men?—He
knows that the Father has "given all things into *His* hands"
(xiii. 3). Is He to be vilified by foul lips?—He can say, knowing
the deeper meaning of the Cross, "Now is the Son of Man
glorified: God shall glorify Him" (xiii. 31-2). Is He to be taken
away from His disciples?—the Father "shall give them another
Comforter" (xiv. 16). Is the prince of this world coming for that
final wrestle in Gethsemane?—He can say, "The prince of this
world hath nothing in Me" (xiv. 30). Are His disciples all to
forsake Him?—He can say, "The Father is with Me" (xvi. 32).
Is He to be crucified?—He can say, speaking of the ultimate
triumph of the Cross, "I, if I be lifted up from the earth, will
draw all men unto Me" (xii. 32).

This then is the explanation of the perfect peace which our
dear Saviour possessed in the dark hour of that supreme crisis.
It was the quiet inward rest which came from His knowledge
and assurance concerning the Divine, the Beyond, the Future,
the Present. This also points the way whereby we ourselves
may come to know a peace which this world can neither give
nor take away.

How much we *need* peace! How earnestly many of us covet
it yet do not seem to gain it! As the Lord's people we feel a
special need of peace arising from the fact of *the world's hostility*

to us. Our attachment to Christ often occasions ostracism, estrangement, even direct persecution. In one way or another we must taste tribulation for the sake of the Name.

Then again we find another special need of peace arising from the fact of *our Lord's long absence.* The apostles themselves were deeply perturbed when the Lord disclosed that He was to leave them. We find Him saying to them, "Because I have said these things unto you, sorrow hath filled your heart." How could it be otherwise with them?—and since then the years have sped away while yet the beloved One remains veiled from us in the unseen.

Yet further, we find a special need of peace arising from the fact of *Satanic opposition.* Our great adversary and his confederate powers never slack off from their efforts to deceive and distract and disturb us. Through circumstances of one kind or another we are constantly tried and tempted. How much we need to know the secret of a peace which nothing can disturb! What would we not give to have a peace like that which the Lord Jesus possessed!

Well, we may have the peace of Jesus Himself, for He says, "*My* peace I give unto *you.*" He has anticipated our need, and made provision for it. Against the world's hostility He says, "In the world ye shall have tribulation; in Me ye have peace." Against the need arising from His own absence He says, "I will not leave you orphans. The Father shall give you another Comforter that He may abide with you for the age." Against Satanic opposition He gives us the assurance, "Be of good cheer; I have overcome"; "Abide in Me, and I in you."

Our Lord well knew, however, that if we were to have a deep and settled peace, such as He Himself had, we must have clear knowledge and unwavering assurance about the four great matters which we have already mentioned,—the Divine, the Beyond, the Future, the Present; for true peace is always founded upon such knowledge and certainty. Thus, in these later chapters of John, We find him completing the wonderful revelation He had come to give pertaining to these very things.

It is in the Lord Jesus Christ, and in Him alone, that we find the knowledge, the assurance, the certitude, which create true peace within us. He brings a revelation of the *Divine* which is marked by a clarity, a unity, an authority, and a finality, such as we find nowhere else. When Philip said, "Lord, show us the Father and it sufficeth us," he was uttering the universal plea of the human heart. "Show us the Father, and it sufficeth us" is what seekers after truth everywhere have asked, and still are asking, however varying the phraseology may be; and Jesus Christ embodies in Himself the one true and full and satisfying revelation of God which has been given to men. Great peoples like those of India are waking up to-day to see that Jesus is indeed the true and final unveiling of the great Heart that beats throughout the universe; and if other nations, like Russia, have in recent days turned against "religion," it is because they have been deceived for generations by a miserable caricature of real Christianity, and have not known the true Jesus Christ. "Show us the Father, and it sufficeth us," cries the unsatisfied soul. The Lord Jesus says: "He that hath seen Me hath seen the Father." "I am the way (by which a man *comes* to the Father); no man cometh unto the Father but by Me." "I am the truth (by which a man *knows* the Father); . . . if ye had known Me ye should have known My father also." "I am the life (by possessing which, a man *possesses* the Father); . . . if a man love Me, . . . We (the Father and the Son) will come unto him and make Our abode with him." Christ is God incarnate: "I am in the Father and the Father in Me." If God be not like Jesus Christ, what *can* He be? Is it crude-sounding to say that God cannot be *better* than He? We can conceive of no moral excellence superior to that which we behold in Jesus Christ, for His is the finality of perfection absolute. In Him we see and know and possess God. We have certitude about the *Divine*. The God revealed in Jesus Christ is such, in His holiness and love, that we may know for certain He will never mock us in our human littleness and weakness. He loves us too dearly. He has *suffered* to save us. To know God thus in Jesus Christ is the first step to a true peace.

But the Lord Jesus gives us equally clear intelligence and assurance about the Beyond, about the Future, and about the Present. As for the Beyond, which has ever been a vexed question in the human heart, He tells us of "the Father's House," and assures His people that He goes to "prepare a place" for them. As for the Future, He promises, "I will come again and receive you unto Myself, that where I am there ye may be also." As for the Present, He covers all the waiting-time until His glorious reappearing by his gracious provision of the Holy Spirit, the Comforter of whom He says, "He shall *abide* with you"; "He shall be *in* you"; "He shall *teach* you"; "He shall *guide* you." On each of these things we can touch only thus briefly here; but these later chapters of John, not to mention all the other recorded teaching of our wonderful Master, are so full of revelation concerning the Beyond, the Future, and the Present, that we gain a knowledge, and (if we are Christ's own) an *assurance*, concerning all the vital issues of life, which fill the mind with restful confidence.

Dear Christian, these are the first things that belong to our peace. We must feed our hearts on the solid comfort of these glorious certainties which our Divine Lord gives to us. When we possess such assurance concerning God and the Beyond, and such a provision for the Future, ought not our peace to be as a full, deep, smooth-flowing river?

Yet wonderful as is the unveiling of truth which our Lord gives to us, there is an even more wonderful way by which He brings peace to His people. This is indicated in that precious pronoun "My"—"MY peace I give unto you." The Lord Jesus here speaks of *imparting His own peace* to our hearts. We are touching now on the most sacred mystery of Christian experience. Our Lord comes not only to *teach* us, but to *indwell* us! This is the crowning revelation. Not only does our Lord give us by His teaching that solid basis of intelligent assurance which is the first essential to real peace, but by indwelling us He pervades the heart with *His own peace*. This is peace Divine!— "the peace of God which passeth all understanding."

"MY peace I give unto you"—turn once more to these closing chapters of John; see how clearly and tenderly the Lord discloses the new truth that He Himself should indwell His people.

"At that day ye shall know that I am in My Father, and ye in Me, and I IN YOU."—xiv. 20.

"If a man love Me he will keep My words, and My Father will love him and We will come unto him, and MAKE OUR ABODE with him."—xiv. 23.

"Abide in Me, and I IN YOU."—xv. 4.

"O righteous Father, . . . I have declared unto them Thy Name, and will declare it, that the love wherewith Thou hast loved Me may be in them, and I IN THEM."—xvii. 26.

While our Lord was here in the body He was *with* his disciples, but not *within* them. Now, however, by the promised diffusion of the Holy Spirit, He abides in the hearts of all His own. Well did He say, "It is expedient for *you* that I go away, for if I go not away the Comforter will not come unto you; but if I go, I will send Him unto you." "He shall be *in you*." "At that day (when the Comforter is come) ye shall know that I am . . . IN YOU." Truly may we sing to the Holy Spirit—

> Sent from the Father, by the Son;
> Come forth our Guide to them to be:
> For Thou, we know, with them art one;
> And WE HAVE THEM IN HAVING THEE.

We may now understand more clearly the terms which our Saviour used when He said, "Peace I leave with you: My peace I give unto you."

Note the two words "leave" and "give"—"Peace I *leave* with you: My peace I *give* unto you." Why the two verbs? Because the peace which Christ makes ours is both a *bequeathment* and a *bestowment*. That which is bequeathed, a legacy, is something which a person leaves *after* his departure. That which is bestowed is something which a person gives *before* his departure. Now the Lord Jesus *bequeathed* peace, as a precious legacy, in the wonderful teaching which He left concerning the Divine, the Beyond, the Present, and the Future. So He said, "Peace I *leave* with you"—peace about all these things. But when He spoke of *His own* peace He could not say, "*My* peace I *leave* with you," for His own peace is of Himself alone. If the very peace of Jesus Himself is to fill these hearts of ours this can only be by a direct *impartation* of His own life to us, a continuous communication of it to us, through the Holy Spirit; so we find Him saying: "*My* peace I *give* unto you."

That Christ indwells His people is a spiritual mystery, but it is an experiential reality; and those who know His abiding presence within them know, in a way which no words can convey, what our Saviour meant when He said, "*My* peace I give unto you."

How then may the indwelling of Christ become a conscious reality to us? The answer is: There must be the continuous, moment-by-moment inter-communication between Christ and the believer which is implied in the words, "Abide in Me, and I in you." For the steady growth of faith and love there must be regular times of communion with Christ, in our private life, and regular meditation upon His words. We cannot always be on our knees; but if our prayer times are regular and real, and we walk with our Lord in faith and love, His communicated life will keep our hearts fresh and fragrant, and free from all disturbing fear. Thus we shall have "the peace of God which passeth all understanding."

> Once I thought I walked with Jesus,
>   Yet such strangeful feelings had,—
> Sometimes trusting, sometimes doubting,
>   Sometimes happy, sometimes sad.
>
> But He drew me closer to Him,
>   Bade my doubts and fearings cease;
> And when I had fully yielded,
>   Filled my soul with perfect peace.
>
> O the peace my Saviour gives!
>   Peace I never knew before;
> And my way still brighter grows
>   As I learn to trust Him more.

"Can I do anything for you?" said an American officer to a soldier who lay wounded and dying on the battlefield, "can I do anything for you?" "Nothing—nothing, thank you." "Shall I go and get you a little water?" "No, thank you; I am dying." "Isn't there anything I can do? Cannot I sit down and write a letter to your friends?" "I have no friends you can write to. There is one thing I would be much obliged to you for. In my haversack, yonder, you will find a Testament. Will you open it? Will you be so good as to turn to the fourteenth of John?— and near the end you will find a verse that begins with the word 'Peace'." The officer turned to the fourteenth of John, and read, "*Peace I leave with you, My peace I give unto you*: not as the world giveth, give I unto you. Let not your heart be troubled, neither let it be afraid." "Thank you, sir," said the dying soldier; "thank you, sir. I have that peace—I am going to that Saviour." In a few moments more the glorified spirit left his poor, wounded frame, and soared away upwards to the hand of infinite love, which, like the hand of Noah from the ark, was reached from heaven, and safely drew him in.

MY JOY

What is our life without joy? Without joy we can do nothing. We are like an instrument out of tune. An instrument out of tune yields but harsh music. Without joy we are like a member out of joint. We can do nothing well without joy, and a good conscience which is the ground of joy.—RICHARD SIBBES.

It is a paradox to the world that there is a joy which can subsist in the midst of sorrow, that the saints have not only some measure of joy in the griefs that abound upon them here, but excellent and eminent joy. That which gives full joy to the soul must be something that is higher than itself. He Who made it can alone make it glad with unspeakable and glorious joy. You that have made choice of Christ for your love, let not your hearts slip out, to renew your wonted base familiarity with sin; for that will bring new bitterness to your souls, and deprive you of the sensible favour of your beloved Jesus. Delight always in God, and give Him your whole heart, for He deserves it all, and is a satisfying good to it. The largest heart is all of it too strait for the riches of consolation which He brings with Him.—ARCHBISHOP LEIGHTON.

MY JOY

"These things I have spoken unto you that My joy might remain in you, and that your joy might be full."—John xv. 11.

THOUGHTS in quick succession leap to mind at the reading of these words, for the words have a many-sided bearing; but that which outstandingly strikes the mind is the unexpected *paradox* here. The deep shadow of the Cross hangs like a pall over everything. In a few hours the beloved Teacher will be transfixed and bleeding upon a criminal's stake. Soon, now, He will be plunged into a sea of suffering the like of which never engulfed another. He Himself knows it. He has foretold His little group of closer friends about it. Yet as He turns His face toward Gethsemane, and knowingly enters the darkness of that supreme sorrow, He speaks of His "*joy*"! He has already spoken to them of comfort, peace, courage, and these were timely enough themes; but to be speaking of *joy* in the face of that unutterable agony! O this amazing joy, this absolutely indestructible, all-victorious joy of Jesus!

But besides the striking paradox here, we see an equally striking *purpose*. "These things have I spoken unto you (with this purpose in view) that *My* joy might remain *in you*, and that your joy might be full." The joy of Jesus within ourselves! What a thought! Yet this is His clear-spoken purpose. Our Lord intends His people to be the possessors and exhibiters of joy. A miserable Christianity is a contradiction in terms, a ludicrous caricature of the real thing. Away with sepulchral sanctimoniousness! A religion which wears grave-clothes begs to be buried, and the sooner the funeral the better! Jesus came to give joy. Mere "religion" may be sombre and dowdy, but true Christianity is more than a religion, it is new life in Christ Jesus—and this new life is a life of joy. "These things have I spoken unto you that My joy might remain in you, and that your joy might be full." See the three things here clearly expressed. Here is (i) Joy *intended* : "These things have I spoken unto you that . . . ." Here is (ii) Joy *imparted* : "My joy . . . in you." Here is (iii) Joy *completed* : "That your joy may be full."

"THESE THINGS HAVE I SPOKEN UNTO YOU. . . ."

Undoubtedly our Lord intends joy for us; but it is vital to realize that our true joy is inseparable from the Lord's *teaching*. He says that He has spoken *"these things"* that we might have joy. What then does our Lord mean by "these things"? He means His teaching in the earlier verses of this chapter. The words, "These things have I spoken unto you," in this eleventh verse, divide the fifteenth chapter of John into two parts. Until now the Lord has been speaking by metaphor—that wonderful metaphor of the vine and the branches; but now, at verse eleven, He passes to plain, unfigurative speaking concerning the relation of His disciples with Himself; and the transition is marked by the words, "These things (the truths expressed by the metaphor of the vine and the branches) have I spoken unto you, that My joy might remain in you, and that your joy might be full." Thus we see not only that our Lord intended that we should have joy, but that our possession of joy is inseparably linked with His teaching about the vine.

What then are the central truths expressed in that metaphor of the vine and the branches? The first great truth is that of *union with Christ*—a vital union with Him, by faith, which makes us so one with Him spiritually that His own life is communicated to us. Apart from the vine the branch is dead, for it has not life of itself; but when the branch is united to the vine it lives, for the life of the vine is communicated to it. Our true joy, then, is *the issue of our union with Christ* ; and apart from this union with Him, the joy of which He speaks can never be ours.

The next great truth is that of *abiding* in Christ. There must be constancy and continuity of union, so that there may be an uninterrupted flow of life from the vine to the branch. This is where many believers fall short and miss the blessing. There cannot be abounding without abiding. This raises the question: How do we "abide" in Christ? The answer is clear. Our Lord says: "If ye keep My commandments ye shall abide in My love; even as I have kept My Father's commandments, and abide in

His love." *Obedience* is the condition of "abiding." What then are the Lord's commandments which we must keep? They are two: (i) faith and love toward Himself, (ii) love toward others. These two things are mentioned again and again in these later chapters of John; and the apostle John himself crystallizes the matter in the following words: "This is His commandment: that we should (i) believe on the name of His Son Jesus Christ; and (ii) love one another, as He gave us commandment. And he that keepeth His commandments *abideth* in Him, and He (Christ) in him (the believer). And hereby we know that He abideth in us by the Spirit which He hath given us" (1 John iii. 23–24).

Thus we see that the joy which the Lord Jesus intends for us is dependent upon an abiding union with Himself—which brings us to the crux of the matter, for it prompts the question: What *is* the "joy" which the Lord here promises? This in turn brings us to that pronoun "My"—"*My* joy," for the joy which the Lord here promises is that which He has Himself. As in other promises which the Lord Himself speaks to us, it is that pronoun "My" which gives significance and lustre to all else.

"THAT MY JOY MIGHT REMAIN IN YOU"

The context makes it quite plain that in using here the expression "*My* joy" our Lord has a double meaning. First, He intends that His disciples, by living according to His teaching, should have the *same kind* of joy as He Himself had. Second, He means that through an abiding union with Himself they should have *His own joy* directly communicated to them by the Holy Spirit.

Take the first of these. He intends that we shall have the *same kind* of joy as He Himself. What then were the constituents of His own joy? Speaking comprehensively, we reverently suggest, they were three. First there was the joy of a *loving, self-sacrificing service for others*, which gave Him, in all that he did, an intensity and fullness of bliss. He lost himself in those for whom He lived and died; and He had that sublime ecstasy of spirit which springs from self-effacing benevolence. Then there was that joy, of which we can have no adequate imagination, which uninterruptedly flowed from His conscious union and communication with the Father; the joy of a cloudless fellowship arising from perfect obedience to the Divine will, perfect harmony with the Divine purpose, and perfect assurance of the Divine approval. Then, also, there was the joy springing from His unswerving confidence in the ultimate triumph of His cause,—"the joy that was set before Him" (Heb. xii. 2).

When, therefore, the Lord Jesus says to us "THESE THINGS have I spoken unto you that *My* joy might remain in you," He clearly means us to understand that if we live according to "these things" which He has taught us, we shall have a joy *like* His own, because our joy will spring from the same *sources* as His own. Just as *He* was one with the Father in a vital spiritual union, and in a fellowship maintained by obedience to the Father's will, *we* are to be one with *Himself* in a vital spiritual union (as set forth in the figure of the vine and the branches), and in a fellowship maintained by a loving obedience to His commands. Just as *He* was motivated by a love which caused Him to lose Himself in self-sacrificing service for others, so *we* are to love others according to the standard of His own word—"Love one another as I have loved you." Just as *He* had the unwavering assurance of ultimate triumph, so are *we* to believe, with an unshakable trust, in His own promise to "come again" in the glorious consummation of His millennial kingdom.

In a word, the joy of Jesus was the joy of what has been called by Henry Drummond "OTHERISM," the joy of living for others. The love of Jesus took Him out of Himself all the while, in self-denying obedience to the Father's will, and in self-forgetting sacrifice for those He had come to save. Even "the joy that was set before Him" was but another expression of His sublime "otherism," for it was the joy of bringing "many sons into glory." Jesus came, and lived, and wrought, and suffered and died, and rose, and lived again, *for others*. His crucifiers were uttering a truth infinitely profounder than they guessed when they said, "He saved *others*: Himself he cannot save!"

OTHERISM! We all have to do with others, and all others have to do with others. "None of us liveth to himself." We are all bound up together in the intricate bundle of our complex life. This matter of "others" is one of the touchiest problems

of human life, and our mortal years can be made either a
"heaven below" or a "hell on earth" by our attitude toward
it. If we will have it, the first secret of joy lies in *otherism*—
living for others. In one of the bedrooms of a certain Christian
home in London, there hangs a little card which bears the words

THE SECRET OF JOY

God first
Others next
Self last.

Is this indeed the secret of joy? Then most of us are sadly
wrong. We think that joy comes by the reverse order; and it
is this mistake which lies behind the worship of wealth, the
passion for power, and the pursuit of pleasure. Verily we are
wrong, as we surely discover sooner or later. The first secret
of joy lies in *otherism*—a going out of one's heart toward others.
Egoism is the supreme enemy of true joy. By many providences
God seeks to break our egoism down. Indeed the very relationships which condition human family life are designed to that
end. John Oxenham thus beautifully puts it:

I, Thou, We, They,
Small words, but mighty,
In their span
Are bound the life and hopes of man.
For first his thoughts of his own self are full,
Until another comes his heart to rule;
For them life's best is centred round their love,
Till younger lives come all their love to prove.

The parental relationships of life, we say, are meant to break
our egoism down. Henry Drummond says, "A man cannot be
a member of a family, and remain an utter egoist." "No greater
day ever dawned than that on which the first human child
was born." Certainly the mother teaches the child; but in a
far deeper way, *is it not the child who teaches the mother?*—and
the little one teaches nothing sublimer than just this very
thing—*otherism*. Parenthood is Divinely designed to initiate
us into the joy-secret of otherism. Mothers! here is a word
for *you*; the secret of joy can be found in the otherism of motherhood. A woman's attitude toward the serving of others at

home can make home either a prison or a paradise. The loving otherism of motherhood was meant to make it a paradise.

OTHERISM! The supreme transition in a human heart is that from "selfism" to "otherism." "One man," says an old Latin proverb, "is no man at all." A "Wayside Pulpit" has it, "A man wrapped up in himself makes a very small parcel!" A life which is always getting and never giving is a Dead Sea. The Lord Jesus says, "Except a corn of wheat fall into the ground, and die, it abideth alone,"—self-preservation the cause of *loneliness*! Then He adds, "but if it die it bringeth forth much fruit"—self-sacrifice the *cure* of loneliness, and the secret behind the joy of harvest!

OTHERISM! Let the word burn into the mind. Like a flame shot into a dark room it suddenly exposes our fundamental error. Like the white flame of a forge let it strike into the thick rust of our selfishness. Oh, if we could but *believe* it, if we would but *receive* it, the first secret of true joy lies just here. We miss joy because we seek it! Joy never comes to those who seek it. Is not the very seeking of joy for its own sake a subtle form of selfishness?—and is not selfishness the very thing that kills joy? Joy is a will-o'-the-wisp to those who run after it; but in some self-forgetting hour when we are touched by another's need, and we sacrifice to give succour, we suddenly find our hearts aflame with a glorious joy that has come unsought! It is thus that we come to know a like joy to that of our dear Lord. In self-sacrificing service for others we discern the marks of His sandals, and follow in the steps of His example, and share His joy. Must we roam afar to find glory? Nay, the secret of pure joy lies behind our own doors, in *otherism*.

> For others' sake to make life sweet,
> Tho' piercing thorns may wound our feet;
> For others' sake to walk each day
> With smile to cheer another's way;
> While in the heart there lies a grave,
> Which makes it hard to be thus brave,—
>   Herein, I think, is love.

Yea, herein is love; and here, paradox though it may sound, is the secret of the joy that excels.

Yet true as may be all that we have said about "otherism," this also is unquestionably true, that when our Lord said "MY joy . . . in *you*," He meant that *His own joy* should be directly imparted to the hearts of His people by the Holy Spirit. Our oneness with Christ is of such a nature that His own life is communicated to us (1 John v. 12, Gal. ii. 20, Col. iii. 4), which means that the *qualities* of that life are imparted too. Thus the Saviour's own joy becomes ours! No wonder our joy is spoken of as "unspeakable and full of glory."

> I have found the joy no tongue can tell
>   How its waves of glory roll!
> It is like a great o'erflowing well
>   Springing up within my soul.

We can now see clearly why the Lord Jesus connected joy with "THESE THINGS" when He spoke about the vine and the branches. He cannot communicate His own joy to a heart which has motives and purposes other than His own. He can never communicate His own joy, for instance, to a heart living for selfish ends, or being at variance with the will of God. But when we are living according to "these things" which He has spoken, that is, when we are spiritually united to Him, walking in glad obedience to the Divine will, and in unselfish love toward all, then our aims and motives and affections are one with His own, and, added to the joy which these things themselves bring us, He floods our hearts with *His own* wonderful joy! Thus our joy is made "full"; and this is why the Saviour says, "These things have I spoken unto you that My joy might remain in you, and that *your joy might be full!*" What it is to have the heart aflame with this pure rapture only those know who have experienced it. We can but say with William Carvosso, one of the early Methodists, "O the blessedness arising from a heartfelt union with a holy God!"

"THESE THINGS HAVE I SPOKEN UNTO YOU THAT MY JOY MIGHT REMAIN IN YOU AND THAT YOUR JOY MIGHT BE FULL."

Take a parting look at the words. They set off in sharp contrast the difference between the artificial joy of the worldling and the true joy of the real Christian.

1. The worldling's joy is *outward*; the Christian's is *inward*. The amusements, business pursuits, entertainment halls, and pleasure resorts, upon which the worldling's happiness depends, are all things external to himself. The weakness of this is obvious. When these external sources of pleasure fail (as sooner or later they inevitably do) the worldling is stranded and destitute. But the Christian has an inward joy which is independent of external circumstances. Our Lord says, "These things have I spoken unto you that My joy might remain IN YOU." "Whosoever drinketh of. the water that I shall give him shall never thirst ; but the water that I shall give him shall be *in him* a well (or *spring*) of water, springing up into everlasting life."

2. The worldling's joy is *changeful*; the Christian's is *constant*. The worldling's joy is fitful and changeful because the things upon which it is dependent are changeful. What restless ups and downs there are! But the true Christian's joy is constant. Our Saviour says, "These things have I spoken unto you that My joy might REMAIN in you." Because we abide in Him His joy all the while abides in us.

3. The worldling's joy is one which he is all the while *seeking*, whereas the Christian's joy is one which he has truly *found*. The worldling's incessant running to one stimulus after another is indication that he is all the time hasting after something which he cannot overtake and permanently possess for himself. How different with the true Christian! "These things have I spoken unto you that My joy might remain in YOU." *We ourselves* possess it. We need not run after a false paradise. We have reached a true Canaan.

4. The worldling's joy at best is merely *human*, whereas the Christian's partakes of the *Divine*. Much of the worldling's pleasure is artificial, for it has to be made for him. He must be amused and entertained; and his pleasure consists in reaction to these things. Some of the worldling's pleasures are definitely degrading. Even the best are bounded by the limitations of his unregenerate human nature. How different again with the Christian! The new life which we have in Christ has awakened new faculties and capacities by which we share the joy of our Lord. "MY joy . . . in you."

O this is life! O this is joy!
My God, to find Thee so!
Thy face to see, Thy voice to hear,
And all Thy love to know!

5. The worldling's joy is based on the inferior principle of *self-seeking*; the Christian's realizes itself through *self-sacrifice*. The worldling's seeming satisfactions come by *getting*, and the more he gets the more he feels he needs, for the simple reason that the more he gets the less he really has. True joy comes by giving, not getting. When our Lord said, "These things have I spoken unto you that *My joy* might remain in you", He was on the way to give *Himself* for us on the cross!

6. The worldling's joy is *superficial*; the Christian's is *deep and full*. This present world caters only for the more superficial elements in human nature. It leaves the deeper depths untouched and unsatisfied. Our Lord's word to His own is "that your joy might be FULL."

7. The worldling's joy fails to survive life's *crises*; the Christian's is *unfailing*. No words are needed to prove this. Hear Lord Byron's pathetic requiem as he lies dying after a life lived for the vain things of the world:

My days are in the yellow leaf,
The flowers and fruits of life are gone:
The worm, the canker and the grief
Are mine alone.

But when our Lord spoke of His own joy, and that which should be in His people, He was on His way to that greatest of all crises. Martyrs have died, saints have suffered, Christians have borne, and they have known through all a joy which is indestructible.

8. The worldling's joy is in *the material*; the Christian's is *spiritual*. George William Curtis tells about Mr. Tidbottom's spectacles, which revealed to those who looked through them what persons really were. Looked at through these spectacles one man was a billiard cue, another was a ledger, another was a bank book, another was a wine goblet. All the worldling's joys gather round the things that are seen and temporal. But the Christian's joy springs from the things which are unseen and eternal. What said our Saviour?—"THESE THINGS have I

spoken unto you that My joy might remain in you"—and it is these spiritual realities which supply our true joy.

9. The worldling's joy is all the while *decreasing*, whereas the Christian's is all the while *increasing*. The older the worldling grows, the less this world has to offer him, until at last, destitute and disillusioned, he sinks into a comfortless grave. The joy of the Christian becomes sweeter, deeper, richer, fuller, as he "abides" in Christ, and as he draws nearer that promised consummation when he will see his blessed Lord face to face, and become perfected in His likeness.

10. In a word, the worldling's joy is *unreal*: the Christian's is *joy indeed*. The poet tells us of the Greek youth who was lured by a beautiful maiden into her forest home. She sang so sweetly, and winked so slyly, and tossed her dainty feet so enticingly, throwing kisses to him all the while from the tips of her deft fingers, that for once he forgot home and loved ones. On and on, and yet on, she drew him, over the rocks and the bogs and the brambles, till, at the end of the day, his chase was given him, and he clasped in his arms a repulsive old sorceress, with a scowl on her face, and a gleam of envy in her eye! This may be the garb of poetry, but it clothes a tragic reality, as many a disillusioned soul has discovered! But there is One who gives real joy; and His people rejoice in Him with "joy unspeakable, and full of glory."

Hear His word again: "These things have I spoken unto you that My joy might remain in you, and that your joy might be full."

> O Christ, in Thee my soul hath found,
>   And found in Thee alone,
> The peace, the joy, I sought so long,
>   The bliss till now unknown.
> Now none but Christ can satisfy,
>   None other name for me:
> There's love, and life, and LASTING JOY,
>   Lord Jesus, found in Thee.

MY REWARD

O that each in the day
Of His coming may say,
" I have fought my way through,
I have finished the work
    Thou didst give me to do."

O that each from His Lord
May receive the glad word,
" Well and faithfully done!
Enter into My joy,
    and sit down on My throne! "

CHARLES WESLEY.

The King there, in His beauty,
    Without a veil is seen;
It were a well-spent journey,
    Though seven deaths lay between.

MRS. A. R. COUSIN.

MY REWARD

"Behold I come quickly; and my reward is with me, to give every man according as his work shall be."—Rev. xxii. 12.

JESUS is coming! He is coming quickly! The announcement falls from the lips of the crowned Christ Himself: "Behold I come quickly; and My reward is with Me." It is a striking and thrilling word. The promise is a double one. There is the promised *return*, and there is the promised *reward*.

THE PROMISED RETURN

"Behold! I come quickly." But how can He be coming *quickly*? Have not nineteen centuries taken their flight since that voice Divine clove the sky? Yea, verily. Can the promise, then, still be true? Most certainly. We are not just toying with words when we point out that the word "quickly" here has the sense of *without delay*; and we must not think that *lapse of time* is necessarily synonymous with delay. Truly there has been lapse of time since the promise broke its gentle thunder on the air of Patmos; but there has been no *delay*.

Much misunderstanding has arisen in one way or another about the second coming of Christ; and by reason of this many have been led into confusion and doubt. This much, however, is surely true, that no honest reader can go through the New Testament without seeing that a personal reappearing of the Lord Jesus, in glory, is clearly, definitely, repeatedly, and altogether unmistakably promised. There may be problems incidental to the doctrine, in which there is room for legitimate difference of opinion, but the central fact is so plainly worded that by no stretch of imagination can the language be exhausted upon the destruction of Jerusalem, upon Pentecost, or upon anything else than a personal, visible, glorious reappearing of the Lord Jesus Himself. In speaking thus we are not defending an opinion; we are simply being honest with the written word of God.

Now much of the misunderstanding concerning this great truth has been caused, we believe, by a failure to recognize sufficiently that the second coming of Christ is presented to us in the New Testament as a *contingent* event—an event, that is, which is to a certain degree dependent upon other transpirings. We cannot here go at length into this, but we will indicate briefly what is in our mind.

When our Lord opened His public ministry His message was that the kingdom of heaven, or the kingdom of God, was at hand. "From that time Jesus began to preach and to say, Repent, for the kingdom of heaven is at hand" (Matt. iv. 17). This was the kingdom which had been foretold in the Old Testament, and for which the Jews were waiting. But the Jews had so doted upon the material aspects of the promised kingdom, and become so blinded to its moral implications, that when the Lord Jesus came, offering Himself as Messiah-King, and enunciating the ethics of the kingdom, they impenitently repudiated Him though He displayed, beyond any misunderstanding, the miraculous credentials of Messiahship; and eventually they sealed their national rejection of Him in the blood of Calvary.

Our Lord's first word on the Cross, however, is "Father, forgive them; for they know not what they do." Can it be that a measure of ignorance may be pleaded for them? Then the avenging hand of retribution upon the nation must be stayed; for a righteous God will not inflict judgment upon either man or nation until guilt has been clearly proved. The nation must be given a second chance to accept Jesus as Messiah. This second chance is given in the period covered by the Acts of the Apostles. The popular idea is that Pentecost, and the narrative in the Acts of the Apostles, marks the instituting of the Christian church. From this we diverge. What we have in the Acts is the renewed offer of the kingdom, and of Jesus as Messiah-King, to the Jews—first to the Jews of the homeland, and then to the Jews of the dispersion, scattered throughout the Roman world. If they have crucified the Messiah through ignorance, then any further plea of ignorance shall now be removed for they shall have a renewed opportunity to accept

Him now that He has risen from the dead and ascended to heaven and poured out the Holy Spirit. They shall have a renewed opportunity accompanied by such signs and miracles as will make it clear beyond all doubt that God is again speaking to the nation.

Now during this period covered by the Acts, the second coming of Christ is contingent upon the national repentance of the Jews, and their acceptance of the Lord Jesus. As an example of the message preached by the Apostles, take Peter's address to the crowd in Solomon's Porch:

"Ye denied the Holy One and the Just, . . . and killed the Prince of Life, Whom God hath raised from the dead, whereof we are witnesses. And now, brethren, I wot that through IGNORANCE ye did it, as did also your rulers. . . . Repent ye therefore, and be converted, that your sins may be blotted out, when the times of refreshing shall come from the presence of the Lord. And HE SHALL SEND JESUS (THE) CHRIST WHICH BEFORE WAS PREACHED UNTO YOU; Whom the heaven must receive until the times of the restoration of all things which God hath spoken by the mouth of all His holy prophets since the world began."

Could anything be plainer? Had the nation then repented and accepted the renewed offer of Jesus as their Messiah, God would have *sent Him back* to them, and the times of "refreshing" and "restoration" would have set in.

But the King and the kingdom were again rejected, first by the leaders of the nation, at the capital, then by the Jews of the dispersion, as recorded in the later chapters of the Acts; and the final pronouncement of the Acts is this solemn, parting word to the Jews: "Be it known therefore unto you that the salvation of God is sent unto the Gentiles, and they will hear it" (Acts xxviii. 28).

The earlier epistles written during this suspense period of the Acts are marked by expectancy of Christ's almost immediate return, as we see in 1 and 2 Thessalonians; but in the later epistles there is a noticeable change. As the further Jewish rejection of the Lord Jesus becomes more and more pronounced, the immediate prospect of the Lord's return recedes. A new factor swings into play—the *Church*, composed of individual Jews and Gentiles alike, without any national distinction whatever. And *now* the second coming of Christ becomes contingent upon a new development, namely, the calling out of a people for Christ from among the Gentiles. Thus, the second coming of Christ now waits "until the fulness of the Gentiles be come in" (Rom. xi. 25).

Yet although the Lord's return is thus contingent, it is not thereby made *indefinite*. In His government of the universe God leaves enough scope for the free action of the human will to make men conscious at all times that they are acting of themselves and by their own intelligent choice; but He does not allow his larger purposes for the race to rest upon the uncertain will of man. Far from it! God foreknows all things; and proceeding from His foreknowledge is His sovereign predetermination of ultimate issues, and His overruling of all intermediate developments to the predetermined end. God foreknew the unbelief of the Jew. Did this unbelief thwart His larger purposes? No; in sovereign super-control He makes even the crucifixion of the nation's Messiah to become the coronation of the world's Saviour! From the dismal ashes of Jewish unbelief there rises up, like a beauteous and stately building, God's further purpose through the Church, and the bringing in of "the fulness of the Gentiles"!

Even so, while in this present prolonged period of grace men are free to accept or to reject Christ as personal Saviour, yet the purpose of God is seen to be sovereign inasmuch as He has given to us, in His prophetic word, great and clear signs whereby we may know when the second coming of Christ is at hand. Moreover, it is our thoughtful persuasion—and one that is shared by many others—that an unprejudiced comparison of Scripture prediction with the present evolution of events gives clear indication that we are on the eve of the glorious reappearing. Yet the very signs which a wonderfully wise God has given to us are such as to give no opportunity for presumption. Who is to say which day He is to come? Who is to say which day he will *not* come? Who is to say when "the fulness of the Gentiles" is brought in to the predetermined point of completion? We are given clear signs; yet the day itself is left in suspense. His coming is *certain some time*. It is *possible any time*. It is *imminent all the time*. It is *likely very soon*. He is coming without delay. "Behold I come quickly!"

THE PROMISED REWARD

Think now of the promised reward: *"My reward is with Me."* These words are a gracious assurance, and at the same time a solemn warning. They are not spoken exclusively to the Lord's own people, but to all men and women, as the wording clearly shows—"My reward is with Me, to give every man according as his work shall be." The word "reward" here has the thought of *requital* in it. The Lord is returning to requite the evil-doer as well as to reward His own servants. Yet the words undoubtedly have special reference to the Lord's own people, and they thus become one of the most inspiring incentives set before us in the word of God.

Look at the pronoun here: "MY reward is with Me." It is this pronoun which gives the promise its supreme glory. Pause for a moment. Think of the One who is here speaking. Think of His transcendent position, His infinite perfections and possessions. How wonderful must be the reward that *He* gives! What is the biggest thing that any other could possibly give compared with the reward which *He* can give, and *will* give?

Look at the word "reward." Again and again in this last book of Holy Writ we find rewards mentioned. But especially the word takes our thoughts to the seven rewards spoken of in Chapters 2 and 3, in the letters to the seven churches; for these were uttered by the Lord Jesus Himself to His own people:

These are the seven rewards promised in the seven letters.

1. *To the church at Ephesus.*

"To him that overcometh will I give to eat of the tree of life which is in the midst of the Paradise of God."

2. *To the church at Smyrna.*

"He that overcometh shall not be hurt of the second death."

3. *To the church at Pergamos.*

"To him that overcometh will I give to eat of the hidden manna, and will give him a white stone, and in the stone a new name written, which no man knoweth saving he that receiveth it."

4. *To the church at Thyatira.*

"He that overcometh and keepeth My works unto the end, to him will I give power over the nations; and he shall rule them with a rod of iron; as the vessels of a potter shall they be broken to shivers. And I will give him the morning star."

5. *To the church at Sardis.*

"He that overcometh, the same shall be clothed in white raiment; and I will not blot out his name out of the book of life but I will confess his name before My Father, and before His angels."

6. *To the church at Philadelphia.*

"Him that overcometh will I make a pillar in the temple of My God, and he shall go no more out: and I will write upon him the name of My God, and the name of the city of My God, which is New Jerusalem, which cometh down out of heaven from My God: and I will write upon him My new name."

7. *To the church at Laodicea.*

"To him that overcometh will I grant to sit with Me in My throne, even as I also overcame and am set down with My Father in His throne."

Now there are two outstandingly significant facts observable in these promised rewards. The first is that in their order and contents they make a remarkable, progressive parallel with Old Testament history right from the garden of Eden to the reign of King Solomon.

The promise to Ephesus is access to the Tree of Life in the Paradise of God. That looks back to EDEN. The promise to Smyrna is deliverance from the second death. That looks back to THE FALL, which brought the curse of death. The promise to Pergamos is the partaking of the hidden manna. That looks back to ISRAEL IN THE WILDERNESS, when God for forty years fed the congregation with bread from heaven. The promise to Thyatira is power over the nations. That looks back to ISRAEL'S CONQUESTS, and, in particular, to the fight with Amalek when Israel prevailed while Moses held high the sacred rod. The promise to Sardis is white raiment. That looks back to THE PRIESTHOOD with their white garments, and the Levitical order. The promise to Philadelphia is that the overcomer shall be made a pillar in the temple of God. That looks back to the building of THE TEMPLE. The promise to Laodicea is joint-occupancy with Christ in his throne. That looks back to THE THRONE of Israel, and especially to Solomon who first reigned with his father, and then became the richest of all Israel's kings.

What rewards these are!—access to the source of life; immunity from death; Divine provision; victory and power; service and purity; worship; and reigning with Christ Himself!

The second thing that strikes us about these rewards is that they climb progressively higher, and the last is the most wonderful of them all: *"To him that overcometh will I grant to sit with Me in My throne; even as I also overcame, and am set down with My Father in His throne."* Can any words express the sublime glory represented in such a promise as this? This is surely the highest reward the human mind can possibly conceive. Thought staggers at such a prospect.

If, however, we would see this reward in its truest light, we must take it in the context of what the New Testament teaches concerning the believer's identification with the Lord Jesus. The mutual identification of Christ and the believer is one of the most fascinating studies in the New Testament. We can only touch upon one aspect of it here, and even that in the briefest possible way. Think for a moment of this great truth from *the believer's* side. We are identified with Christ in seven ways.

First, we are identified with Him in His *nature*. Peter speaks of us as "partakers of the Divine nature" (2 Pet. i. 4). When by faith we become united to Christ, His own life is imparted to us. In Colossians iii. 4, Paul speaks of "Christ Who *is* our life."

Second, we are identified with Christ in his *character*. The fundamental purpose of our salvation is that we should be made into His likeness. "Whom He (God) did foreknow, He also did predestinate to be conformed to the image of His Son." The life of Christ being imparted to us, the *qualities* of that life are also imparted; and thus we come into increasing oneness with His character.

We are identified with Him, also, in his *experiences*. He says, "My peace I give unto you," and again, "My joy . . . in you." He experienced *the world's hatred*, and so do we. "If the world hate you, ye know that it hated Me before it hated you." Our Lord *suffered*, and "*we* suffer with Him" (Rom. viii. 17). Our Lord experienced in a most wonderful way *the love of the Father*, and in John xvii He prays "That the love wherewith Thou hast loved Me may be in *them*."

Again, we are identified with Christ in His *relationships*. On the morning of His resurrection He says, "Go to My brethren, and say unto them, I ascend unto *My* Father, and *your* Father, and to *My* God and *your* God." In Hebrews ii. 11 we read: "He that sanctifieth (Christ) and they who are sanctified (ourselves) are all of one, for which cause He is not ashamed to call them *brethren*."

Still further, we are identified with Christ in *service*. He says, "As My Father hath sent Me even so send I you" (John xx. 21). "Go . . . and, lo, I am with you alway" (Matt. xxviii. 20). "Workers together with Him" (2 Cor. vi. 1). What a priceless dignity and privilege is this!

We are further identified with Christ in His *possessions*. Romans viii. 17 tells us that we are "joint-heirs with Christ." In 1 Corinthians iii. 23, Paul says, "All things are yours, and ye are Christ's, and Christ is God's." In John xvii. 22 our Lord says, in His great prayer to the Father, "The glory which Thou gavest Me, I have given them." Who shall tell the blessedness contained in such words as these?

Finally, we are identified with Christ in His *reward*. "To him that overcometh will I grant to sit with Me in My throne, even as I also overcame and am set down with My Father in His throne." To what height of thought does such a word as this lift the mind! Note the pronoun, "*My* throne." There is a clear distinction here made between "*My* throne" and "My *Father's* throne." By the Father's throne is meant the eternal throne of the Deity. As the eternal Co-equal of the Father, the Son evermore shares this throne. That is why, in Revelation xxii. 3, where the final state of eternal glory is described, we read of but the one throne, "the throne of God and of the Lamb." Yet even so, the Son of God now shares the Father's throne in a new way, for besides being the eternal

Son of God, He is now, and "unto the ages," the "Son of Man" Who "overcame" and bore His victorious and glorified human nature up to the throne of Deity and is "set down" with the Father "in His throne."

When our Lord says "To him that overcometh will I grant to sit with Me in *My* throne," He is referring to His Messianic throne and His millennial reign. When He comes again, in power and glory, then will He lift His resistless rod over the nations, and unfurl the banner of His world-wide reign. The evil one shall be interned in the bottomless abyss. Evil shall be completely subjugated. Righteousness and peace shall be dispensed to the nations. Christ Jesus shall reign upon the Davidic throne which has been promised and covenanted to Him. A chastened and renewed Israel will send His messengers of enlightenment and peace throughout the earth. Science and invention, scholarship and art, shall all devote themselves to noblest ends. War shall be done away; and the throne of David's greater Son shall be supreme.

It will be wonderful to live under that reign, yet it will be more wonderful still to reign *with* Him; and this is what Jesus promises. "To him that overcometh will I grant to *sit with Me in My throne.*" What a promise! What a reward! What a consummation! What an incentive! The promise is to "the *overcomer.*" Are all believers "overcomers"? Let him think twice who would answer a dogmatic "yes" to this question. The letters to the seven churches, to say the least, suggest otherwise to an unprejudiced reader. Our standing in Christ is no artificial position of immunity and privilege. As there are degrees of punishment so there are degrees of reward. One is made ruler over ten cities, another over five. "One star differeth from another star in glory."

We would make ourselves rather clearer on this point. We have no sympathy with that theory which is known as the "partial" rapture. We do not believe that when Christ returns He is only coming for a certain number of His people and that the others will be left on earth when the vials of God's wrath are poured out. We have no sympathy with it because we find no Scripture for it. We believe that when our Lord returns, *all* who are truly His, washed in His precious blood, regenerated by the Holy Spirit, and thus savingly united with the Lord, will be raptured away to "meet the Lord in the air."

Surely 1 Corinthians xv. 51 settles that point, without there being any need for the quoting of other verses. Mark the distinction made by the double occurrence of the word, "all". "We shall not *all* sleep, but we shall *all* be changed". And *when* are we "all" to be thus changed or transfigured? Is it at different times, or is it all simultaneously? The very next verse tells us: "In a moment, in the twinkling of an eye, *at the last trump*; for the trumpet shall sound, and the dead shall be raised incorruptible, and we shall be changed."

No, we do not believe in a "partial" rapture. Quite apart from such clear pronouncements as 1 Corinthians xv. 51, 52, we simply cannot conceive of our Lord's coming for only a *part* of His mystic "body" and "bride" and "temple," the Church (for we believe that the metaphor of "bride" refers to the Church, over against some who teach otherwise). When the "fulness of the Gentiles" shall come in, and the elect members of the "body of Christ" are numerically completed, then our Lord will return for His own. And since His coming is actually contingent upon that completed inbringing of the elect, can we possibly think that He is coming for only a part of them?

All true believers will be "caught up . . . to meet the Lord in the air." All will have their part in that "first resurrection" and transfiguring translation. All will have their place at the "Marriage Supper of the Lamb," and share in the millennial reign of David's Greater Son. Yet even that does not mean that there will be no difference of honour and distinction and reward among believers. There will be *degrees* of reward. "One star differeth from another star in glory." One shall be made "ruler over ten cities," and another "ruler over five cities." None will lose reward for service; but there will be greater and lesser rewards. *Salvation* is a matter of pure unmerited grace on God's part, and of simple faith alone on our part; but *reward* is a matter of faithfulness in service and suffering for the Lord. Oh, may all of us "so run that we may obtain"! With a loving zeal like that of Paul's may we "press toward the mark," for "the prize" of that supreme reward—

"To him that overcometh will I grant to sit
with Me in My throne; even as I also overcame,
and am set down with My Father in His throne."

Part Two

—"*OUR PART*"

It was one of the immeasurable evils which the Roman Catholic Church inflicted on Christendom, that it held constantly before the eyes of the Church the exhausted, suffering, agonized form of Christ on the Cross—fastened the thought and imagination of Christian men on the extremity of His mortal weakness—and so deprived them of the animation and the courage inspired by the knowledge that He is now on the throne of the Eternal. A similar loss may be inflicted on ourselves if our thoughts are imprisoned within the limits of the earthly life of Christ, and if we do not exult in His resurrection and in His constant presence in the Church. The historic Christ is the Object of memory; the present, the living Christ, is the Object of faith, the Source of power, the Inspiration of love, the Author of salvation. Christ must be infinitely more than an august and pathetic tradition to us. He is the Contemporary of all generations.—R. W. DALE.

"He died," saith the Cross; "my very name
Was a hated thing and a word of shame;
But since Christ hung on my arms outspread,
With nails in His hands and thorns on His head,
They do but measure—set high, flung wide—
The measureless love of the Crucified."

" He rose," saith the Tomb; " I was dark and drear,
And the sound of my name wove a spell of fear;
But the Lord of Life in my depths hath lain
To break Death's power and rend his chain;
And a light streams forth from my open door,
For the Lord is risen; He dies no more."

ANNIE JOHNSON FLINT.

MY REDEEMER

"I know that my Redeemer liveth, and that He shall stand at the latter day upon the earth: and though after my skin worms destroy this body, yet in my flesh shall I see God: Whom I shall see for myself, and not another; though my reins be consumed within me."—Job. xix. 25–27.

THERE is much in the book of Job to oppress the spirit. The sky is draped with clouds; the atmosphere is heavy. In the end, to be sure, the clouds break up, the miserable mists melt away, and the sun smiles down from a sky of unflecked blue: but we are a while before we get to this, and the heart sighs by reason of the clinging mists. Yet midway, even here, there comes at least one gladdening break. Suddenly there is a rift in the clouds, and a flood of glory bursts through, transfiguring the drab scene for the moment, and prophesying an ultimate issue in clear shining. Just when things seem darkest and dreariest the inspired sufferer exclaims, "I know that my Redeemer liveth, and that He shall stand at the latter day upon the earth: and though after my skin worms destroy this body, yet in my flesh shall I see God; whom I shall see for myself, and mine eyes shall behold, and not another; though my reins be consumed within me."

How gladdening indeed—to change the metaphor—is the note of ringing certitude here, "I *know*"! It is the man who can say "I know," about the things which fundamentally matter, who possesses the secret of true peace and joy and satisfaction. It is the man who can say "I know," about God and ultimate issues, who finds streams in the desert, and sings songs in the night, and carries within his breast the indestructible pledge of a compensating consummation, however painful the postponement and deplorable the present. As Paul walks to the executioner's block he rests his heart on this invulnerable certainty: "I know Whom I have believed, and am persuaded that He is able to keep that which I have committed to Him against that day." Even Death cowers before the steady eye of certainty. It was the man who could say, "I know that my Redeemer liveth" who could say, "Though He slay me, yet will I trust in Him." Doubt is destructive. Speculation is vague Inference is uncertain. Mere supposition is shifting sand. Certainty alone is solid rock beneath our feet; and no wise man will build on anything other than this. Alas, how flimsy are the standards by which multitudes to-day meander through life! "I think," "I assume," "I hope," "I imagine," "I suppose," "I guess," "I dare say." However many pleasures such people pack into their mortal span, they never know the meaning of real heart-rest and abiding satisfaction. Their pleasures may be passionate, but they are paltry in reality.

To hear many wiseacres to-day—and all too many of them have climbed into Christian pulpits—one would think that certainly about the vital matters of the soul is no longer possible. The most devastating disease that blights modern Protestantism is its chaotic uncertainty about the fundamentals of the Christian faith. Need we wonder that much present-day preaching is like beating the air, and that the public pass the pulpit unheeding by? Give us back the thunder of the prophet, and the certainty of the first witnesses, and the people will listen.

That wise old master of Christian apologetics, Paley, has a sagacious and discerning word to the effect that we should never let what we do *not* know disturb our faith in what we *do* know. However much we may yet learn that we do not know at present, it will not make what is true to be *un*true. We may not yet understand the mysteries of suffering and the presence of evil, but these mysteries, baffling and tremendous as they are, do not destroy the basic and central truths of the Christian faith. The Son of God has become incarnate, and the Bible has been written, and the Holy Spirit has come, to witness in the hearts of Christ's people, that we might have a triple cord of certainty about Divine realities.

Some time ago I came across a book, *From Agnosticism to Christianity*, in which the writer says that the first thing which drew him from agnosticism to Christian faith was the difference between the characteristic expression of his anti-Christian books and that of the New Testament. The favourite type of expression among his agnostic and sceptical authors was, "Since such and such is most probably the case, *we may therefore assume . . .*" The characteristic word of the New Testament is "We *know*." The true Christian, to-day, can say, with far more historical knowledge than ever Job had, "I know that my Redeemer liveth, and that He shall stand at the latter day upon the earth."

It is good to know that Job could speak in such terms of certainty regarding God. The buffeted patriarch had all manner of doubt-suggesting circumstances with which to contend. Wave after wave of trouble broke over his head. Heart-breaking domestic calamities suddenly robbed him of life's tenderest joys. Loathsome physical disorders made him an object of revulsion, and a burden to himself. Added to all this, he was harassed by the exasperating verbosity and controversiality of would-be comforters who were as undiscerning as they were dogmatic. Yet from this tempestuous sea of adversity there rises up in solemn grandeur this solid rock of unshakable conviction—"I know that my Redeemer liveth, and that He shall stand at the latter day upon the earth; and though after my skin worms destroy this body, yet in my flesh I shall see God." Yea, and what glorious certainty this is which Job possessed! Here is (i) the supreme reality of the present—"My Redeemer liveth." Here is (ii) the supreme prospect of the future—"He shall stand at the latter day upon the earth." Here is (iii) the supreme miracle of all history—"And though after my skin worms destroy this body, yet in my flesh shall I see God."

MY REDEEMER LIVETH

The occurrence of the word "redeemer" here is striking in the extreme. There can be no questioning that the reference is to God; and when we reflect that the book of Job, and not Genesis, is probably the earliest-written book of our Scriptures, we realize that so far as we have any record this is the first time in history that a human soul looked heaven-ward and called God "Redeemer." In that word the faith of Job cleaves its way to the very heart of the Eternal. His faith is as sublime as the word is daring and glorious. In the presence of life's darkest hour and most baffling enigma Job awakes to his supreme discovery of God.

We do not suggest for a moment that Job included in the word all that we now see in it of evangelical significance, but, on the other hand, the context undoubtedly indicates that with the spiritual intuition of the prophet, Job had grasped far more of its evangelical significance than some modern commentators are inclined to grant.

The Hebrew word here translated "redeemer" is *goël*, a word of fairly frequent occurrence and fascinating usage in the Old Testament. From its original signification, namely to *release* that which is bound, it develops the further meaning to *deliver*, to *redeem*, to *avenge*. Under the Mosaic economy these obligations of delivering, redeeming, and avenging, devolve upon a person's nearest kinsman, so that the word now comes to stand for the kinsman-vindicator. The more important elements in the law regarding the kinsman-vindicator, or kinsman-redeemer, are given in Leviticus xxv, from which the following lines are quoted:

"And if a sojourner or stranger wax rich by thee, and thy brother that dwelleth by him wax poor, and sell himself unto the stranger or sojourner by thee, or to the stock of the stranger's family; after that he is sold he may be redeemed again; one of his brethren may redeem him. Either his uncle, or his uncle's son, may redeem him, or any that is nigh of kin unto him of his family may redeem him; or if he be able, he may redeem himself."

"If thy brother be waxen poor, and hath sold away some of his possession, and if any of his kin come to redeem it, then shall he redeem that which his brother sold."

The following two quotations are taken from Numbers xxxv and Deuteronomy xix:

"Speak unto the children of Israel, and say unto them: When ye be come over Jordan into the land of Canaan, then ye shall appoint you cities to be cities of refuge for you, that the slayer may flee thither which killeth any person at unawares; and they shall be unto you cities for refuge from the avenger (*goël*), that the manslayer die not, until he stand before the congregation in judgment."

"But if any man hate his neighbour, and lie in wait for him, and fleeth into one of these cities: then the elders of his city shall send and fetch him thence, and deliver him into the hand of the avenger of blood (*goël*), that he may die. Thine eye shall not pity him, but thou shalt put away the guilt of innocent blood from Israel, that it may go well with thee."

These excerpts from the legal code of Israel lay down three requirements pertaining to the *goēl*:

1. He is to be the next of kin, or a near kinsman.

2. He is to redeem his brother, and his brother's inheritance, according to ability.

3. He is to be the avenger of fatal violence against his brother.

These are the three predominant stipulations in the Mosaic institution concerning the *goēl*—kinsmanship, redemption, vindiction; and this is the word which Job uses of God. We will not insist that Job included these three ideas in his uses of the word, though the strong presumption is that he *did*, for such conceptions as those involved in the word *goēl* are of great antiquity; and, indeed, why should Job so deliberately and emphatically employ this special word here at all unless he intended to apply its distinctively redemptive content to God? We cannot but feel that Job, with the inspiration of a heaven-born faith, had apprehended, in advance, far more evangelical truth than perhaps we are at first disposed to allow.

This, at any rate, is the word which Job here uses; and what a stupendous word it becomes when predicated of God! Lo, the Eternal, the infinite Creator, becomes my Kinsman, Redeemer, Vindicator! Surely there is Divine revelation as well as human aspiration in Job's inspired affirmation, "I know that my Redeemer liveth."

"My *Kinsman*"—what a name for God! Yet it is true to fact. In the incarnate Son, born of the virgin, bone of our bone, flesh of our flesh, the Eternal has taken to Himself a blood-relationship with us. "Veiled in flesh the Godhead see! Hail the incarnate Deity!" He is made "in the likeness of men" —not just the likeness of *a* man, but *all* men. He is not simply a Jew. He is not a Greek, a Roman, an Englishman, a German. He is the universal Man: the blood of the whole race courses in His veins. He is every man's Brother. He is my near Kinsman!

And He is my "*Redeemer*"—the One who pays my ransom price, emancipates me from bondage, buys back my forfeited inheritance, avenges me of my adversary, restores my birth-right, and reconstitutes me a free son of God. Yea, wonder of all wonders, He Who is my Redeemer is also the redemption-price itself, for He gives *Himself* to redeem me. Well says the apostle, "Ye are bought with a price."

He is also my "*Vindicator*"—my Vindicator against the Law which justly held me under condemnation, for He has taken my place, and fulfilled on my behalf all my accumulated obligation to the Law, so that in Him I now stand justified and acquitted. "It is God that justifieth: who is he that condemneth?" He is my Avenger against Satan, the binder and accuser. He is my Vindicator before the holy throne of God; for, having paid the price of my redemption, and having effected my justification, and having freed me from the bondage of Satan, He takes away the alienation and rebellion from my heart, and gives me the Spirit of adoption whereby I cry "Abba Father." What a word is this—"My Kinsman—Redeemer—Vindicator!"

"My Redeemer *liveth*." Yes,. he liveth! Job could say it. Still more may we say it who live in the light of the Easter miracle. Yet hark back to Job again. See his victorious faith. Read between the lines, and supplement the words. "I know that my Redeemer liveth. His manifestation may be yet future, but His actual existence as my Redeemer is a present reality. At the latter day He shall stand upon the earth; but even *now* He lives on high and has my cause in hand." Christ's birth at Bethlehem was not His beginning! Before the world had its beginning the Word had His being. The world is *from* the beginning. The Word was *in* the beginning. Truly could the Old Testament saint say, "My Redeemer liveth." Yet in the full blaze of resurrection light the Christian believer can take Job's words upon his lips and invest them with an immeasurably richer significance. The long-anticipated Redeemer has taber-nacled among men, has wrought salvation, has despoiled the adversary and conquered death, has brought life and immortality to light through the Gospel, and has become "able to save to the uttermost all them that come unto God by Him." Thank God, Christianity is not built upon a coffin lid! Our ensign bears no skull and cross-bones! "Now is Christ risen from the dead, and become the firstfruits of them that are fallen asleep." A dead Christ is no Saviour. The sufferer of Golgotha has proved Himself the victor of Easter morning. The sun that set in blood on Calvary has ascended in glory over Olivet.

> Jesus lives! thy terrors now
>   Can no longer, Death, appal us;
> Jesus lives! by this we know
>   Thou, O Grave, canst not enthral us.
>   Hallelujah!

But who shall speak the sweetness, the priceless worth, of the possessive pronoun here? "*My* Redeemer liveth." After all, what means this mighty doctrine of the Divine *Goël* unless I can say that He is *my* Redeemer? But when once I can call Him mine!—Ah, it is only those who have learned to call Him "*my* Redeemer" who know the ineffable bliss of that word.

> I know that my Redeemer lives,
> What comfort this sweet sentence gives!
> He lives, He lives, who once was dead,
> He lives, my ever-living Head.
> He lives, He reigns in yonder skies,
> He lives, and *I* from death shall rise.
> He lives, my mansion to prepare,
> He lives, to bring me safely there.
> He lives, and will return in power,
> He lives, He comes, O golden hour!
> He lives, all glory to His Name,
> He lives, my Jesus, still the same!
> O the sweet joy this sentence gives,—
> "I know that my Redeemer lives"!

"HE SHALL STAND AT THE LATTER DAY UPON THE EARTH"

The more one weighs Job's great utterance the more one becomes impressed with its extraordinariness. The patriarch seems to have been under some extraordinary impulse of the Spirit, and to have realized in his own mind that he was about to make a momentous and transcendent declaration, for he prefaces his declaration in a peculiarly solemn manner. Hear him:

"Oh that my words were now written! Oh that they were printed in a book! That they were graven with an iron pen and lead in the rock for ever!"

Job is so anxious that his testimony should be everlastingly perpetuated that he refers, apparently, to every mode of

recording known in his time. First he sighs that his words
might be *written*. Then, unsatisfied by any mere stray recording
of his words, he says, "Oh that they were *printed in a book*," by
which, it scarcely need be said, he does not refer to printing and
bookbinding in the modern sense, but to the tracing out of his
words upon a roll,—a roll made of papyrus, or palm leaves, or
other similar substance then in use, and carefully preserved like
other such rolls. Nay, Job goes still further. He judges his words
such as to be worthy of time-enduring commemoration, and
wants them "graven with an iron pen in the rock." He desires
the characters of his record to be cut deep, with an iron chisel,
into some imposing rock, so that generations to come might
behold them, and ponder. Yet even this does not suffice the
man's deeply stirred soul. His words must be "lead in the rock
for ever," that is, the deep incisions made in the rock by the
chisel must be filled with lead so that the memorial might be
conspicuous and enduring to the remotest reach of the years.

Truly, Job himself was movingly conscious that he was making a profound pronouncement here, and it must have seemed
an almost unbearable irony to him that the uttering of it seemed
wasted on desert air. Had he but known it, his "Witness on
high," the very One whom, with sublime audacity of faith he was
daring to claim as his "Redeemer," had determined that Job's
words *should* be preserved for ever, and in an unspeakably
grander way than ever crossed the imagination of the good man.
Not only have his words been written, and written in the
greatest of all books; they have been immortalized by the Spirit
of God, and inscribed for evermore in what William Ewart
Gladstone magnificently named "The Impregnable Rock of
Holy Scripture."

Gaze, ye sons of men, at Job's rock-hewn message to posterity.
"My Redeemer is the Living One. He shall stand at the latter
day upon the earth." The words, "He shall stand," have the
sense of "He shall arise"—that is, He shall arise in vindication
of Job's cause. The words "at the latter day" are, literally,
"at the last." They suggest not so much a literal, final *day* as a
final *issue*. "At the last, and in the final issue, my Redeemer,
the Living One, shall arise, upon the earth, for my vindication."

And what *now* of Job's grasp of evangelical truth? Are we
not listening here to a *prophet*? "Is not Job also among the

prophets?" What now will those say who tell us that when Job spoke about his coming vindication he was merely referring to the restoration of prosperity to him, as recorded in the last chapter of this old-time drama? They are on the horns of a dilemma. If they do justice to Job's language here they must admit that Job is looking into distant futurity: yet if they weaken the language, and say that Job was simply referring to his restored prosperity of a few months or years later, they must explain the strange fact that Job most definitely did not expect any such return of prosperity, for he expresses his expectation of dying by his disease. We are driven to the conclusion that Job had caught a glimpse of those eschatological glories which have been the inspiration of saints from antediluvian Enoch down to the present day. The Living One who has already been to the earth to redeem is returning to reign, to stand up, upon the earth, in final vindication of right, and of them that are His true people. We do not come within measurable distance of saying that Job foresaw the two advents of the coming Redeemer, but he certainly saw the final outcome, the ultimate vindication, the conclusive solution of the mystifying problem of suffering, and something of the glory of that tremendous consummation for which we ourselves also wait, with the open page of the New Testament before us.

"IN MY FLESH SHALL I SEE GOD"

Here is the climax. This is faith absolutely victorious. Let disease and death do their worst, even they shall be made the servants of that ultimate restitution. The man of faith sees this with shining and steady eye as being involved in the righteous government of the world by a holy God. It must be. It shall be. It is a moral necessity. "Though, after my skin worms destroy this body, yet in my flesh shall I see God." The word "worms" does not occur here in the Hebrew, nor need it in the English. It gives a needlessly gruesome tinge to Job's noble exultation. Job uses the word "skin" here because his malady was one which showed itself outwardly in obnoxious skin disorders. We may render his words: "After my skin has been thus destroyed, yet from my flesh shall I see God." It is a superlatively triumphant outburst.

Considered from a purely grammatical standpoint, the Hebrew words translated as "in my flesh" present a problem. The Hebrew preposition *min* may be translated as *"from"* (in the sense of *from out of*), or as "apart from," or as "in." If we read it, *"Apart from* my flesh shall I see God," then Job is telling us that though his body be destroyed, yet apart from his flesh he will see God in the spiritual realm. If we use our English preposition "in," and slightly rearrange the sequence, we may read, "I shall see *God in my flesh*"; in which case Job is pointing to the incarnation of the Redeemer, and telling us that the heavenly Redeemer would one day come in human flesh. If we read it *"From* my flesh shall I see God," meaning *from out of*, then Job is telling us of a coming resurrection which will restore to him in perfected form his decomposed body, so that in his own body, and with his own eyes, he would see God. If Job is *thus* to see God, *from out of* his body, it involves that Job himself must be *in* the body; and this is the sense given to the words in our Authorised Version, "In my flesh shall I see God."

What then is the true sense of the words? We submit that though this grammatical difficulty exists, there can be no missing the implication of the words when viewed contextually. If Job were only going to see his Redeemer apart from the flesh, in the spiritual realm, then certainly for this there would be no need for his Redeemer to stand at the latter day upon the earth. As for the other suggested meaning—that Job would simply see God, from the spiritual realm, clothed in human flesh like that of other men, how then explain Job's dilating fondly on the fact that with his own eyes, and not those of another, he would look on his Redeemer?—"Whom I shall see for myself, and not (the eyes of) another." Nay, beyond doubt, this chastened sufferer of long ago has his eye on the coming resurrection and glorification of the saints. The flash of expectancy in his eye is the reflection of the glory-light which he has suddenly seen away out beyond the sunset—"in my flesh shall I see God, whom I shall see for myself (really and actually), and mine eyes shall behold, and not (the eyes of) another!" "Beloved, now are we the sons of God, and it doth not yet appear what we shall be: but we know that when He shall appear, we shall be like Him, for we shall see Him as He is."

O glorious hope! with this elate,
Let not our hearts be desolate,
But strong in faith, in patience wait,
    Until He come.

And what further? Why this: we have examined some of the terms in this triumphant manifesto, and have seen something of their far-reaching implication, yet we miss the most poignant significance and thrilling conception of all unless we view the words in the sweep of their larger context, and in relation to the soul of Job himself.

Read this nineteenth chapter again. Read it thoughtfully, and yet quickly enough to get into the rush of Job's passionate and heart-rending expostulation with his three cruelly unsympathetic friends—one of whom, Bildad, has just been labelling Job as false, and saying, "The light of the wicked shall be put out . . . his remembrance shall perish from the earth . . . he shall be driven into darkness . . . he shall neither have son nor nephew among his people, nor any remaining in his dwellings"—not to mention other bitter things. In an uttermost anguish, broken-spirited Job now pathetically pleads with them in the words of this nineteenth chapter, one of the most touching passages in all literature, a few verses of which run as follows, according to Dr. Robert A. Watson's rendering:

Behold, of wrong I cry, but I am not heard;
I cry for help, but there is no judgment.
He hath stripped me of my glory,
And taken my crown from my head.
He hath put my brethren far from me,
And my confidants are wholly estranged from me.
My kinsfolk have failed,
And my familiar friends have forgotten me.
They that dwell in my house count me a stranger;
I am an alien in their sight.
I call my servant and he gives me no answer,
I must entreat him with my mouth.
My breath is offensive to my wife,
And my ill savour to the sons of my body.
Even young children despise me;
If I would rise they speak against me.
My bone cleaveth to my skin and to my flesh,
And I am escaped with the skin of my teeth.

It is in the misery of all this that Job despairingly implores:

> Have pity upon me, have pity upon me, O ye my friends,
> For the hand of God hath touched me.
> Why do ye persecute me as God,
> And are not satisfied with my flesh?

Poor Job! Added to that which is inflicted by Divine permission is the alienation and contempt of men. Bildad's cruel sword has plunged its jagged edge deep into his already torn soul. Job struggles to bring his friends to some realization of what all his bitter sufferings mean to him. If he must die without one sign of Heaven's relenting, he longs that at least some human friend might stand beside him. Let one at least say, "Job, dear friend, perhaps you are sincere, and are being misjudged." But nay, the poor sufferer's pleading is wasted. Not one of those grim faces relaxes. What then? With circumstances and providence and familiars and friends and all others against him he is flung once for all upon God with a desperate sense of the need of HIM. And lo, from his abyss of grief he gazes upward, through eyes burning with an intensity of agony, into the face of God, to make the all-transforming and tranquillizing discovery which he wanted graven into the rock for ever:

> "I know that my Redeemer liveth, and that He shall stand at the latter day upon the earth; and though after my skin this body be destroyed, yet in my flesh shall I see God: Whom I shall see for myself, and mine eyes shall behold, and not (the eyes of) another: my reins be consumed within me."

Job has at last found solution and satisfaction in this great fact: Over against problem and pain in the present there is a sovereign Vindicator of the righteous, who is himself the pledge of restitution yet to be when all wrongs shall be righted, in a day of resurrection light and glory. And is not this great fact that upon which we ourselves must rest to-day? We cannot explain the enigmas, the problems, the sufferings, the mysteries, of our present lot. Considered by itself this present life often seems bitterly unfair and hopelessly baffling. Here is a man who would do service for God and for his fellow men, but he is stricken down with some fell disease which holds him bedfast for weary years: while here is another whose every thought is selfishness and vice, and he walks abroad in unimpaired health. Here is a young man conscious of gifts and powers, and of an inward urge to some noble vocation, but he is without due social prestige, without monetary reserves, and is frustrated while others without either the gifts or the urge are pushed before him. Here is a man of wisdom, integrity, and benevolent heart, who would have been a benefactor to thousands had he possessed material means; while here is another of grovelling ideals who possesses more than he can count, and he wastes his substance in riotous living.

O how endlessly could one multiply such instances! All over the world there are men and women good and true who are mercilessly thwarted and beaten back by ironic inequalities. All through the churches there are saints longing to do some big and noble thing for their Lord, yet they are dashed back panting and breathless, crushed and seemingly mocked, by wave after wave of frustrating circumstances. Is not this true of all of us in some way? Oh, what we would do! . . . but that incurable illness lays us low, that crushing blow falls and smashes our hopes, that gnawing trouble wastes our strength, that irretrievable disappointment plunges us into darkness, that life-long poverty, that adversity, that impediment, that affliction, cuts us off from serving Christ as we would.

What can we say about it all? And what can we say about the wars that curse the race, the devilish cruelties that are perpetrated, the colossal evils that breathe the fumes of hell across the earth? What can we say about it all? We can say what Job said, and say it with the confirmatory evidence of a historical background which Job never possessed. We know that there is a Living One on high who is the sovereign and final Vindicator of righteousness and of the righteous, and that in the Person of the Lord Jesus Christ He will certainly stand up, upon the earth, in a day of judgment and glory which is the goal of Biblical prediction.

Fellow Christian, be comforted. The righteous *Goël* on high knows full well those things which we would do but cannot. He takes the will for the deed, where the will is really sincere, even as He did in the case of David—"Thy son shall build the house for My Name," yet "forasmuch as it was in thine heart to build an house for My Name thou didst well." This is a comforting thought indeed. God knows, and understands; he counts the deed of love to Him as good as done; and in that day yet to be He will confess us, will vindicate us, before the universe, and give us at last the opportunity which we have sought.

What a day that will be! See how Job anticipates it, "My reins be consumed within me" (not "*though* my reins" as in the Authorised Version. The italicised word "though" does not occur in the Hebrew). "My *reins be consumed within me*," that is, "I burn with intense longing." O for the coming of that sunlit day! My heart and my flesh cry out for the living God, and for the appearing of the Lord Jesus in the glory of His second advent! This is surely the true attitude of all Christ's own; for with that brightest of all sunrises the perfect day shall break across the earth, and the shadows shall flee away. "Even so, come, Lord Jesus."

> So I am watching quietly
>   Every day;
> Whenever the sun shines brightly
>   I rise and say,
> Surely it is the shining of His face!
> And look into the gates of His high place,
>   Beyond the sea,
> For I know He is coming shortly
>   To summon me,
> And when a shadow falls across the window
>   Of my room,
> Where I am working my appointed task,
> I lift my head to watch the door— and ask,
>   If He is come;
> And the Angel answers sweetly,
>   In my home,
> Only a few more shadows,
>   And He will come.

MY SHEPHERD

I notice that some of the flock keep near the shepherd, and follow whithersoever he goes, without the least hesitation; while others stray about on either side, or loiter far behind, and he often turns round and scolds them in a sharp, stern cry, or sends a stone after them. As there are many flocks in such a place as this, it is necessary that they should be taught to follow, and not to stray away into the unfenced fields of corn which lie so temptingly on either side. Any one that thus wanders is sure to get into trouble. The shepherd goes before, not merely to point out the way, but to see if it is practicable and safe. He is armed in order to defend his charge, and in this he is very courageous. There are wolves in abundance; and leopards and panthers, exceeding fierce, prowl about the wild wadies. They not unfrequently attack the flock in the very presence of the shepherd, and he must be ready to do battle at a moment's warning. Some sheep always keep near the shepherd, and are his special favourites. Each of them has a name, to which it answers joyfully; and the kind shepherd is ever distributing to such, choice portions which he gathers for that purpose. These are the contented and happy ones. They are in no danger of getting lost or into mischief, nor do wild beasts or thieves come near them. The great body, however, are mere worldlings intent upon their mere pleasures or selfish interests. They run from bush to bush searching for a variety of delicacies, and only now and then lift their heads to see where the shepherd is, or rather, where the general flock is. Others, again, are restless, climbing into bushes, and even into leaning trees, whence they often fall and break their limbs. These cost the good shepherd incessant trouble.
—W. M. THOMSON, D.D., *The Land and the Book*.

MY SHEPHERD

"The Lord is my Shepherd; I shall not want. He maketh me to lie down in green pastures. He leadeth me beside the still waters. He restoreth my soul. He leadeth me in the paths of righteousness for His Name's sake. Yea, though I walk through the valley of the shadow of death, I will fear no evil; for Thou art with me; Thy rod and Thy staff they comfort me. Thou preparest a table before me in the presence of mine enemies. Thou anointest my head with oil; my cup runneth over. Surely goodness and mercy shall follow me all the days of my life; and I will dwell in the house of the Lord for ever."—Ps. xxiii.

THIS EXQUISITE composition is one of the most treasured and beautiful portions in the Book of Books. It merits to the full the many eulogisms which have been uttered concerning it. Says one: "What the nightingale is among birds, that is this Divine ode among the psalms." Says another: "This is the pearl of psalms, the soft and pure radiance of which delights every eye." Says another: "What the opening rosebud is among the flowers of the garden, that is this psalm among the writings of David." As a literary product it is "par excellence." As a spiritual message it is "multum in parvo." The half-dozen verses would leave but a small blank in the page if they were blotted out; yet suppose as one has suggested, that all the translations which have been made of them into many languages, all references to them in literature, all remembrance of them in human hearts, could be effaced, who shall measure the blank, or calculate the loss?

Henry Ward Beecher says: "It has charmed more griefs to rest than all the philosophy of the world. It has remanded to their dungeon more felon thoughts, more black doubts, more thieving sorrows, than there are sands on the sea-shore. It has comforted the noble host of the poor. It has sung courage to the army of the disappointed. It has poured balm and consolation into the hearts of the sick, of captives in dungeons, of widows in their pinching griefs, of orphans in their loneliness.

Nor is its work done. It will go singing to your children and my children, and to their children, through all the generations of time."

Nor is the beauty of this psalm like that of many other elegant compositions which lose their charm through familiar usage. It comes to us as the voice of a human heart; yet the words are fragrant with the breath of God. It is the testimony born of a man's experience; yet the Spirit of inspiration has breathed into it, and imprinted upon it an undying beauty which appeals to human hearts everywhere. The lines are as fresh as if they were written yesterday. The dew of perpetual youth is upon them. Every time we read them they come to us with the freshness of the morning and the brightness of the sunrise. The petals of this rose never fall; the bloom never pales, and the fragrance never departs. This is the alpha star of its constellation; its glory excelleth; and its tender shinings never fail the wanderer in the night. This is the prime jewel of royal David's treasury. This is the choicest chord on the harp of Israel's sweetest singer. This is the clearest and sweetest of all the crystal cascades that gush from Zion's heights to refresh the weary travellers below.

To have written this psalm is one of the highest honours ever given to man. I would rather have written this one short piece than have conquered nations, like Alexander or Caesar. I would rather have been the penman of these few sentences than have evolved philosophies, like Aristotle or Spinoza. This twenty-third psalm has brought more benign and lasting comfort to human hearts than all the spectacular victories of warriors and all the elaborate systems of philosophers. Libraries have grown and perished; yet these lines remain. There is nothing like them in all the books of the East. They make themselves at home in every language; and, as one has written, "they touch, inspire, comfort us, not as an echo from three thousand years ago, but as the voice of a living friend. The child repeats them at his mother's knee; the scholar expends on them his choicest learning; the plain man loves them for their simplicity as much as for their beauty; the Church lifts them to heaven in the many-voiced chorus; they fall like music in the sick man's ear and heart; the dying Christian says: 'That is *my* psalm,' and cheers himself with its words of faith and courage as he enters the dark valley."

The author of *Ecce Homo* says that this psalm is "the most complete picture of happiness that ever was or can be drawn. It represents that state of mind for which all alike sigh, and the want of which makes life a failure, to most; it represents that heaven which is everywhere if we could but enter it, and yet almost nowhere because so few of us can." O that we might learn and prove the secret of this psalm!—for then would the days of our mourning be ended; then would we have beauty for ashes, the oil of joy for mourning, and the garment of praise for the spirit of heaviness; then would our peace be as a river, our confidence as the immovable hills, and our experience fulness of joy in believing.

So, then, we turn again to this immortal little psalm. But it is no detailed study of each verse which we have in mind. It is the main idea of it which captures our imagination, namely, the shepherd character of Jehovah. We want simply to bring this out in a kind of "impressionist" way, first the divine, and then the human aspects of it.

1. THE DIVINE ASPECT

This twenty-third psalm conveys a unique message about our heavenly Shepherd by its very *position*. Psalms xxii, xxiii, and xxiv are a kind of trinity in unity.

Psalm xxii is all about the suffering Saviour:

"My God, My God, why hast Thou forsaken Me? They pierced My hands and My feet. They part My garments among them, and cast lots upon My vesture. Thou hast brought Me to the dust of death."

Psalm xxiii is the psalm of the living Shepherd:

"The Lord is my Shepherd; I shall not want. He leadeth me. He restoreth my soul. Yea, though I walk through the valley of the shadow of death, I will fear no evil: for Thou art with me; Thy rod and Thy staff they comfort me."

Psalm xxiv is the psalm of the exalted King:

"Lift up your heads, O ye gates; and be ye lift up, ye everlasting doors; and the King of glory shall come in. Who is this King of glory? The Lord strong and mighty, the Lord mighty in battle."

Thus in Psalm xxii the dying One is our *Saviour*. In Psalm xxiii the living One is our *Shepherd*. In Psalm xxiv the exalted One is our *Sovereign*. Psalm xxii is the Good Friday psalm. Psalm xxiii, telling of the living and abiding Shepherd, is the Easter morning psalm. Psalm xxiv is the Ascension day psalm. We thus have in these three psalms—the *cross*, the *crook*, and the *crown*.

Now parallel with these three psalms there are three places in the New Testament where our Lord's shepherd character is specially referred to. First there is John x, where the emphasis is upon the Shepherd's giving His own life for the sheep—*as in Psalm xxii*.

"I am the good Shepherd. The good Shepherd giveth His life for the sheep. I lay down My life for the sheep."

Second, there is Hebrews xiii. 20–21, where we see the Shepherd risen and perfecting that which concerns his flock—*as in Psalm xxiii*.

"Now the God of peace, that brought again from the dead our Lord Jesus, that great Shepherd of the sheep, through the blood of the everlasting covenant, make you perfect to do His will."

Third, there is 1 Peter v. 4, where we see the Lord at His reappearing in glory bringing crowns of reward—*speaking of Psalm xxiv*.

"And when the chief Shepherd shall appear, ye shall receive a crown of glory that fadeth not away."

Thus our Lord's shepherd work has three aspects indicated by the adjectives "good," "great," "chief," and corresponding with Psalms xxii, xxiii, and xxiv. Thus also we see that the twenty-third psalm is the central piece of a sublimely beautiful triune fore-picturing of the Lord Jesus as the true Shepherd of His people.

And now, in the next place, we gratefully observe *the main concept* of the psalm. That which makes the word "shepherd" so wonderful here is its being linked to the Lord Himself. How safe for evermore are the sheep of such a Shepherd! The word "Lord" is here printed in capitals to indicate that the Hebrew word is *Jehovah*. Also, the copula "is" appears in italics. This is because it does not appear in the original. Need it be here in the English? Should not the words read as the exclamation of joyous discovery? "JEHOVAH—MY SHEPHERD!" Shall we who have found the Saviour ever forget the hour when *we* made the supreme discovery, when we first looked up into the face of our Lord and exclaimed, "Jesus—*my* Saviour!"? Was it not somewhat after this sort that David was feeling when he exclaimed, "Jehovah—my Shepherd!"?

"JEHOVAH my Shepherd!" Is there not something sublimely daring here? That name "JEHOVAH" was inviolately sacred to the Hebrew. It was the incommunicable name of Israel's covenant-keeping God, never used of another. It was only spoken once a year, we are told, and even then only by the High Priest when he went into the Holy of Holies.

Yet when David connected that word "shepherd" with the name "Jehovah," he was completing, under the overruling guidance of the inspiring Spirit, a striking Old Testament revelation of God, in connection with the name "Jehovah." Reading through the Old Testament books we find certain words attached to "Jehovah" which, together with the name, convey a wonderful revelation of God.

There are seven such instances:

Jehovah-jireh . . .	"The Lord will provide" (Gen. xxii. 13–14).
Jehovah-rapha . .	"The Lord that healeth" (Exod. xv. 26).
Jehovah-shalom . .	"The Lord our peace" (Judges vi. 24).
Jehovah-tsidkenu . .	"The Lord our righteousness" (Jer. xxiii. 6).
Jehovah-shammah . .	"The Lord ever-present" (Ezek. xlviii. 35).
Jehovah-nissi . . .	"The Lord our banner" (Exod. xvii. 8–15).
Jehovah-ra-ah . .	"The Lord my shepherd" (Ps. xxiii. 1).

Jehovah is distinctly the redemption name of Deity; and in these seven compound Jehovistic titles, God is revealed as meeting every need of man in his fallen state. Is not that a wonder of Divine grace and revelation? We cannot think of one need or yearning in these needy hearts of ours which is not here prescribed for. God is the All-in-All of those who truly know and love Him.

Now it is a singularly impressive fact that all these seven wonderful Divine provisions indicated in these seven compound Jehovistic names are gathered up in this twenty-third psalm!

Take them in the order just given:

Jehovah-jireh
(The Lord will provide)—"I shall not want" (literally "I shall lack nothing").

Jehovah-rapha
(The Lord that healeth)—"He restoreth my soul."

Jehovah-shalom
(The Lord our peace)—"He leadeth me beside the still waters."

Jehovah-tsidkenu
(The Lord our righteousness)—"He leadeth me in the paths of righteousness."

Jehovah-shammah
(The Lord ever-present)—"I will fear no evil for Thou art with me."

Jehovah-nissi
(The Lord our banner)—"Thou preparest a table before me in the presence of mine enemies."

Jehovah-ra-ah
(The Lord my Shepherd)—"The Lord is my Shepherd."

Is it this which gives the psalm its incomparable appeal? Happy are they who know this all-sufficient Shepherd, Saviour, Guide and Friend! "*Jehovah*—my Shepherd!"

And what comforting spiritual application of this we may make! If Jehovah Himself be my Shepherd I may say without any presumption: "I shall not want." To say less would not be humility but unbelief. "I shall not want"—the Prayer-Book version brings out the full force—"Therefore can I lack nothing."

Why, that happy inference, "I can lack nothing," is the key to the whole psalm. "He maketh me to lie down in green pastures"—so I shall not lack *provision*. "He leadeth me beside the still waters"—so I shall not lack *peace*. "He restoreth my soul"—so I shall not lack *restoration* if I faint or fail. "He leadeth me in the paths of righteousness"—so I shall not lack *guidance*. "Yea, though I walk through the valley of the shadow of death I will fear no evil"—I shall not lack *courage* in the dark hour. "For Thou art with me"—I shall never lack *His dear presence*. "Thy rod and Thy staff they comfort me"—I shall not lack true *comfort*. "Thou preparest a table before me in the presence of mine enemies"—so I shall not lack *protection, preservation*, and *honour*. "Thou anointest my head with oil"—I shall never lack *joy*, of which anointing is the symbol. "My cup runneth over"—I shall not lack fulness of *blessing*. "Surely goodness and mercy shall follow me all the days of my life"—so I shall not lack the Divine *favour* as long as I live on earth. "And I will dwell in the house of the Lord for ever"—I shall not lack a heavenly home when my earthly journeyings are done.

"The Lord is my Shepherd; I shall not want." Since the Authorised Version was made in 1611, a real difference in meaning has steadily developed between the word "want" and the word "lack," the word "want" now meaning desire, and "lack" indicating a real need or deficiency. Using the words in this, their modern sense, we cannot say with the little girl who innocently misquoted the first verse of the psalm, "The Lord's my Shepherd; *I've got all I want!*" but we can and do rejoice in the fact that no real need shall be left unsupplied.

2. THE HUMAN ASPECT

Take one further look at the words. They are *the language of a man*, the expression of a human heart; and, as such, how revealing they are! It has been truly said that in the Bible, as in the person of the Lord Jesus, the Divine and the human are blended in such close union as to be inseparable. The human writers of the Scriptures were not merely passive instruments involuntarily monopolized to bring about a written revelation of God. It was not just by the pens or lips of these men that God spoke, but by the men themselves. Thus we find Peter saying, "Holy men of God spake as they were moved by the Holy Ghost." The Divine inbreathing is there, giving the message authority and finality; yet the human vehicle gives the complexion of his own personality and experience to it. Were it an angel who had said, "The Lord is my Shepherd," it would have brought little consolation to these frail human hearts of ours. Were it even God Himself who had declared by a voice from the skies, "The Lord is your Shepherd," it would not have had the tender appeal which the word has in coming to us by the voice of a brother man, weak and needy as ourselves.

"The Lord is my Shepherd"—this is the language of *ripe experience*. The twenty-third psalm wings our thoughts away back to David's youth, when he shepherded the flocks on Bethlehem's hills; but the psalm itself is no composition of David's youth. The marks of maturity are upon it. It bears the stamp of experience. David has long ago said good-bye to boyhood and youth. He has "enemies." He has had dark experiences, and can speak of "the valley of the shadow of death." He has lived long enough to know life and to prove God. Through varied scenes and changeful episodes he has found that God is faithful. Jehovah has proved Himself the true Shepherd, the all-sufficiency of the trusting heart. Experience is the greatest of all teachers though his fees are sometimes heavy. There is no knowledge of God so convincing and assuring as that which comes through first-hand experience of His reality and faithfulness. When David exclaims "The Lord is my Shepherd", he is voicing a discovery which was born through experience. Have we ourselves thus proved God?

"The Lord is my Shepherd"—this is the language of *humble confession*. In acknowledging the Lord as his Shepherd David takes the place of the sheep, humbly acknowledging thereby his ignorance and need of teaching, his proneness to wander, and his need of guidance, his helplessness in himself, and his need of protection, his utter dependence upon the Lord for preservation and sustenance and every good. This is the position *I* must take too if I would call Jesus "*my*" Shepherd.

"The Lord is my Shepherd"—this is the language of *peaceful assurance*. If the LORD be David's Shepherd there need be no anxiety. The divine Shepherd will care for His own. And if He is *my* Shepherd I may indeed say, "I shall lack nothing." What peaceful assurance we enjoy when our hearts have welcomed Jesus as Saviour! As the sheep belongs to the shepherd, so we belong to Him. We are His by purchase-price, for the good Shepherd bought us with His own precious blood. Being thus purchased and possessed, we are led by His Spirit, fed by His word, and kept by His power.

"The Lord is my Shepherd"—this is the language of *grateful love*. David, the one-time shepherd youth, was now king of Israel, and the greatest power of his day. He had much that he could sing about. He might have sung of the famous past, of his illustrious achievements, of his rise to power and fame. No, the veteran king, looking back over the years, sees a light, a meaning, a watchful, gracious Presence, which now calls forth the love of his heart. He would sing his choicest song. What or whom shall it be about? With a heart overflowingly full of grateful love, he breaks forth into the song that has awakened more echoes in human hearts than any other—"The Lord is my Shepherd. . . ."

"The Lord is my Shepherd"—this is the language of *appropriating faith*. After all, it is that precious pronoun which makes these words so wonderful. "The Lord is *my* Shepherd." Elsewhere God is revealed as a Shepherd to His people in general; but David, with appropriating faith, makes it personal and individual—"The Lord is *my* Shepherd." All life becomes wondrously different when we learn to say from the heart: "Jesus, *my* Shepherd."

> Heaven above is softer blue,
>   Earth around is sweeter green,
> Something lives in every hue,
>   Christless eyes have never seen;
> Birds with gladder songs o'erflow,
>   Flowers with deeper beauty shine,
> Since I know as now I know—
>   I am His, and He is mine.

Years ago at a fashionable gathering in the West End of London, a noted actor and an aged clergyman were present. Someone suggested that the gifted actor should recite the twenty-third psalm, to which the actor obligingly responded.

With mellifluous voice, he so artistically rendered the psalm that his hearers were mentally transported to the shepherd scenes of the Orient; and when he finished there was much applause. It was then insisted that the aged minister also should recite the psalm. Reluctant, under the spell of the actor's elocution, the minister held back, but finally yielded to pressure. Certainly there was little of the actor's flawless elocution; but there was something else which brought an atmosphere of strange quiet into the room. It was quite evident, as the aged man proceeded, that he was not so much describing a scene as voicing an experience; and when he sat down there was an impressive silence. The actor then got up and said words like these: "My friends, we have been most impressed. Our old friend has been speaking to our hearts. You see the difference between himself and myself is this: *I* know the *psalm; he* knows the *Shepherd.*"

What of ourselves? "The Lord is *my* Shepherd"—God grant that we also may be able to take that precious pronoun upon our grateful lips!

MY HELPER

Fly from it (covetousness) as you would fly from the most cruel and destroying adversary. O Sirs, to be angry because God is bountiful to others; to frown because God smiles upon others; to be bitter because God is sweet in His dealings with others; to sigh because God multiplies favours and blessings upon others; what is this but to turn others' good into our own hurt, others' glory and mercy into our own punishment and torment? If this be not to create a hell in our own hearts I am much mistaken.—THOMAS BROOKS.

MY HELPER

"Let your conversation be without covetousness; and be content with such things as ye have; for He hath said: I will never leave thee, nor forsake thee. So that we may boldly say: The Lord is my helper, and I will not fear what man shall do unto me."—Heb. xiii. 5–6.

THANK God, here is something we may say "boldly." In these days, when the knees of theological doctors bend beneath a burden of doubts, and orthodox creeds are bashfully apologized for in the hesitating syllables of uncertainty, this breath of healthful dogmatism comes as a refresher to wearied spirits.

"We may boldly say"—no, no, we are warned, we must *not* "boldly say." We must on no account be dogmatic lest we offend the æsthetic sensitiveness of the cultured "can't believe" fraternity around us; and we make no mistake about this, that in being thus warned not to be dogmatic, we are really being told not to be definite about anything. Far better not insist that Jesus really rose from the grave than offend one of these doubting Thomases of our day. If by dogmatism were meant strong-headed self-opinionativeness, then we would surely join issue in decrying it; but this genteel plea for polite indefiniteness—well, we can only reply to it by saying, with a certain ministerial friend of ours, "Far better be dogmatic than phlegmatic!"

"We may boldly say"—thank God, here is something well *worthy* of being said boldly. "We may boldly say: The Lord is my helper." What comfort there is here! It brings a sympathetic Divine friend to stand with us right down amid the homeliest as well as the largest concerns of our earthly life. It comes to us as a promise of God, to strengthen the weak hands, to confirm the feeble knees, and to say to them that are fearful "Be strong; fear not!"

There is something peculiarly comforting in this word "The Lord is my *helper*." Is there anything we human beings need

more than this very thing *help*? Few things are more important, more determining, than the sources from which we
receive our help. Let the mind wander back through child-
hood and youth; or think of that fateful first stepping out
into "grown-up" life, business adventure, family responsibilities: how seriously has our life been affected by the
sources to which we have looked for counsel and direction,
and assistance in other ways! The same is true of all our life.
Happy is the man who knows a Divine Refuge, and who can
boldly say "The Lord is my helper!"

"The Lord is my helper"; we must take this word in its
context, for thus it is seen to be the affirmation of intelligent
faith. It will be seen that this last chapter of Hebrews consists of final admonitions and instructions, each complete in
itself, and without any reference to argumentative sequence.
Verses 5 and 6 go together, and constitute an independent
entity.

"Let your conversation be without covetousness; and be content with such things as ye have; for He hath said: I will never
leave thee, nor forsake thee; so that we may boldly say: The Lord
is my helper, and I will not fear what man shall do unto me."

The word, "The Lord is my helper," is both preceded and
followed by an Old Testament reference. Going before it we
have: "I will never leave thee, nor forsake thee" (Joshua i. 5).
Coming after it we have: "I will not fear what man shall do
unto me" (Ps. cxviii. 6). Indeed, this word itself, "The Lord
is my helper," is part of the quotation from this psalm; so
that it now comes to us with a kind of double assurance from
both the Old Testament and the New. Thus, examining this
affirmation of faith in its context, we see (i) its foundational
connection with the Old Testament scriptures, (ii) its unique
expression of the Divine faithfulness, (iii) its intended influence
in the experience of the believer, namely, to destroy covetousness and fear. In other words, we are led to consider its basis,
its terms, its purpose.

THE BASIS

"He hath said: I will never leave thee, nor forsake thee:
so that we may boldly say: The Lord is my helper." The

basis on which true faith builds is the word of God. Note
the argument here—"He hath said . . . we may say." This
is the logic, the authority, the sheet-anchor, of faith. Thus
faith is not mere presumption. It grounds every "we may
say" in a "He hath said." It is the characteristic of doubt
to turn affirmations into interrogations. It turns every "He
hath said" into "Hath he said?" and every "We may say"
into "May we say?" Doubt, therefore, by its very nature, is
both dishonouring to God and dissatisfying to man. Faith,
on the other hand, having duly ascertained by reasonable
proof that God has indeed spoken, plants its feet unfalteringly
on the firm foundation of the faithful Divine word. The
pronoun "He" in our text is emphatic. It has the force of
"He Himself hath said." The fact that it is God Himself who
has spoken is everything to faith. However startling may be
the word, if it be truly the word of God Himself, that is all
faith asks.

> Faith, mighty faith, the promise sees,
>   And looks to that alone;
> Laughs at impossibilities,
>   And cries: It shall be done!

"He hath said"—see here *the implication regarding the Old
Testament.* To the Lord Jesus and the apostles the Old Testament was "He hath said." We turn over the pages of our
New Testament, and what do we find? The writers are continually *quoting* the Old Testament, but they never once *query*
it. No candid mind can fail to be impressed with the witness
of the incarnate Lord and his apostles to the Divine authority
of the Old Testament. When modernist-minded people turn
on us and say it is preposterous to believe that every sentence
in the Old Testament is the word of God they are begging
the question. The Old Testament is a diversity in unity.
Besides its direct didactic pronouncements, in precept and
promise and prediction, there are large tracts given to historical records in which are included the sayings and doings of
men and women and nations which are held up before us not
as examples to be emulated but as warnings to be heeded.
All that is in the Old Testament is there by Divine design and
for a Divine purpose, but that is far from saying that every
sentence is—or is meant to be taken as—a direct didactic

communication from God. Nay, in parts of the Old Testament the devil himself is quoted; yet while his words are certainly not to be taken as the word of God, they are nevertheless included as being necessary to the Old Testament message as a whole. The inspiration of the Old Testament involves that its histories and prophecies are true, and that those direct declarations which are given as "thus saith the Lord" are to be taken as being indeed the word of God. The book is a harmonious whole both structurally and spiritually; and its message as a whole is a "He hath said."

Again and again the Lord Jesus and the New Testament writers preface their quotations from the Old Testament simply by the words "He saith"—meaning, of course, that *God* saith. This is enough for ourselves. We know that there are those in our churches and in our pulpits who disparage the Old Testament, but we are not of their fraternity, and do not wish to be; nor do we think any true lover of the Lord Jesus will wish to be. We have yet to see how these men can claim sincere allegiance to the infallible Lord and yet dishonour the book which He declared to be the word of God. We believe they are of the synagogue of Satan, for in destroying faith in the word of God they are doing the work which Satan has been doing ever since he said to Eve in Eden "Hath God said?"

Brethren, let us take our stand with our Divine Lord and His Spirit-taught apostles, believing that "He hath said." However much further evidence may be forthcoming to confirm the Old Testament, whether it be geological, archæological, historical, or of any other kind, there are those who, with deep-set antipathy toward it, will still cling to the badly battered bulwarks of Modernism. Like the Brahmin who saw through a microscope that the water of his sacred Ganges was contaminated with disease-germs, and then smashed the microscope to pieces rather than admit the exposure of his superstition, so these men will refuse clear light rather than yield even a grudging admission of error. Where the Old Testament is "rightly divided," intelligently quoted, and dealt with fairly—a treatment it seldom receives to-day—it carries its own vindication. We cannot do without it. New Testament faith has an Old Testament basis; and that basis, we are glad to believe, is truly a "He hath said."

But to come to a pleasanter consideration, see also, in our text, the expression of *an important spiritual principle.* "He hath said . . . we may say." What was it that God said? and to whom did He say it? He said: "I will never leave thee, nor forsake thee"; and He said it to Joshua. By what right, then, do we appropriate the gracious pledge as belonging to ourselves? The answer to that question is found in 2 Corinthians i. 18–20.

"But as God is true, our word toward you was not yea and nay, . . . for all the promises of God in Him are yea, and in Him amen, unto the glory of God by us."

Note carefully the words "But as God is true." Both in the Revised Version and in the Authorised (in italics) the word "as" occurs, but should not. It does not occur in the original. Nor should it appear in the English. It obscures the sense. Paul is making a direct statement, namely, "God is true." The Greek word here translated "true" is the word commonly given as "faithful." That is how it should appear here, as indeed it does in the Revised Version. Thus, in these two verses, Paul first makes the statement "God is faithful," and then shows how the Divine faithfulness has been demonstrated—"for all the promises of God in Him (Christ) are yea, and in Him amen, unto the glory of God by us." All the promises God ever made are honoured by Him in Christ, for Christ is in Himself the fulfilment of them all. All the promises of God become our property in Christ. They are ours in Him by redemption right. The promises may have been given originally to Jacob, Moses, Joshua, David, and others; but there was a larger thought behind them than that which merely concerned the individual; and they are now ours in Christ. By this principle the comforting assurance vouchsafed to Joshua belongs to *me.* "He hath said: I will never leave thee, nor forsake thee: so that *we* may boldly say: The Lord is *my* helper."

Ponder the *graciousness* of this assurance. It is a double pledge. Our Lord will neither "leave" us nor "forsake" us. That word "leave," in common usage, means to depart from; but the Greek word here must not be thus limited. Weymouth renders it, "I will never *let you go*," which keeps close to the literal sense. The Revised Version has it "I will in no wise *fail* thee," which perhaps best gives the inclusive idea. Then the second word, "forsake," means that God will never abandon or desert us. Thus God pledges that He will never let us go, and never give us up. What a promise!

See, also, the remarkable *emphasis* here. No less than five negatives are heaped together in the Greek, to confirm the gracious pledge, and to give us strong consolation from God who cannot lie. A literal translation is scarcely possible. It would run in this way, "No, not will I fail thee; nor, no, not will I forsake thee." A more emphatic, energetic, and absolutely final guarantee could not be given in any language under the sun. One can only struggle to bring out the full force of it in the English by translating with a double negative in each line,

> I will never, *never* fail thee;
> I will never, *never* forsake thee.

What a priceless gem we have here! Far better be heir to a promise like this than to the biggest earthly fortune ever heard of! How can our eyes feast on such a pledge of undying Divine love without weeping tears of adoring gratitude? Besides being comprehensive and emphatic, as we have seen, it is individual, unconditional, and unalterable. There is a remarkable word ascribed to Socrates: "Since God be so careful for you, what need you to be careful (anxious) for anything yourselves?" We have not asked the permission of Socrates to spell the word "God" in this quotation with the capital "G". We are quite sure that had he lived in the light of the Christian revelation he would have spoken his devout word with truer meaning, and of the one true God who has revealed Himself as our great Father in Christ. "Since God be so careful for you, what need you to be anxious for anything yourselves?" "I will never, never fail thee, and never, never forsake thee."

> The soul that on Jesus hath leaned for repose,
> He will not, He will not desert to its foes.
> That soul, though all hell should endeavour to shake,
> He'll never, no *never*, no NEVER forsake.

THE TERMS·

Have we not rejoiced to behold the promise of our God? Well then, having thought upon what "He hath said," let us now see what "we may say" in consequence. We may boldly say, "The Lord is my helper."

The word "helper" has an appeal all its own. It comes from a Greek word which is a compound of two verbs, the one meaning *to cry* (for help), and the other meaning *to run*: so that the compound word gives the picture of one ready to run at the cry of another. Such is our tender-hearted Lord toward His loved ones. Says Puritan Thomas Brooks: "You know the tender father, the indulgent mother, the careful nurse, they presently run when any of them hears the child cry, or sees the child in any danger or distress; so when God sees His poor children in any danger or distress, when He hears them complain and cry out of their suffering, their bonds, their burdens, their oppressions, their dangers, He presently runs to their relief and succour."

Consider, then, the solid comfort of this great fact, troubled believer, that the Lord Himself is thy helper, and thou canst say this boldly, for it is grounded in His own sure word. Wipe the mist of uncertainty from thine eye. Let limping doubt become leaping faith. Let this Magna Charta of thine eternal security turn sighing into singing and repining into rejoicings. Think over some of thy Lord's attributes in His condescending rôle as thy helper, and it will be as the very wine of heaven to make the heart glad.

He is an *almighty* helper. "Who is like Him in all the world?" asks our Puritan friend. "When friends cannot help, when power cannot help, when policy cannot help, when riches cannot help, when princes cannot help, when parliaments cannot help, yet then God can and will help His people." With such an almighty helper we can keep fear beneath our heel. My soul, who is like unto "the God of Jeshurun who rideth upon the heaven in thy help"? Are we cast down into some valley of adversity? Then truly we can say, "I will lift up mine eyes to the hills. From whence cometh my help? My help cometh from the Lord which made heaven and earth." How we can know that we have such an almighty helper, and yet allow ourselves to be the easy prey of carking care is a strange phenomenon which must surely be a perplexity to onlooking angels! What is thy need, thy fear, thy trouble, believer? Can anything be too hard for thine almighty Lord? Say it boldly: "The Lord is my helper; I will not fear."

Remember that the Lord is a *constant* helper. This was David's comfort in a day of distress: "God is our refuge and strength, a very present help in trouble." Our Lord is not a fair-weather companion only. When the dark hour comes when the storm beats about us, when the grievous blow falls, He is the Friend that "sticketh closer than a brother." He is our all-sufficient stand-by "through thick and thin," as the common saying has it. Ah, in such an hour as we most need help we may boldly say, "The Lord is my helper," for has He not said "I will never, *never* fail thee, and never, *never* forsake thee"?

What is more, the Lord is a *present* helper. Turn to David's word again: "God is our refuge and strength, a very *present help* in trouble." Our Lord is not merely a distant spectator of our concerns, far removed from us in a far-off sky. He is a "present" help. When a loved one lay seriously ill, and death seemed near, telegrams were sent to relatives. Some of the replies were, "Sorry cannot come." How oft when we most need our human loved ones they cannot get to us! It is never thus with our heavenly helper. Not only is our Lord a "help," and a help in "trouble," and a "present" help; He is a "*very*" present help—as though He would draw still closer to our hearts than even the word "present" conveys. How the Divine love heaps up these tender words of assurance!

Still further, the Lord is an *immediate* helper. He is not only present in the sense of being on the spot; He is present in point of time. We can always boldly say it in the present tense, "The Lord *is* my helper." It is good to be able to raise our Ebenezers and to say, "*Hitherto* hath the Lord helped us"; yet help in the past is little comfort if I am stranded at present and cannot say that the Lord is my helper here and now. Even the promise of future help is little good unless I get the help that will save me now. What comfort to a drowning man to tell him that the life-boat will put out to rescue him in a week? What comfort to a starving beggar to tell him that some kind friend will send him a loaf in a month? Thank God, we have a helper who is both "very" present and *ever*-present. We may boldly say: "The Lord *is* my helper." Fellow-Christian, think well over this—He is thy helper *now*.

Must we not also add that the Lord is an *individual* helper? Most certainly is He the helper of His people and their cause considered collectively: but He is more than the God of the multitude. Each of His people may boldly say, "The Lord is *my* helper." Thrice-blessed word—"*my* helper"! God's Elijahs can go on the strength of this meat for more than forty days! If we feed on such cheering fare as this we shall never find ourselves under the Juniper tree. Three times over in three verses in Isaiah xli we have these words spoken to the fearful: "Fear not, I will help thee." Why will we persist in thinking that although God can meet the needs of others our own needs are somehow of a specially difficult kind even for God to deal with? We will readily agree that God can do many wonderful things for others; but when an inward Voice tells us that He can do the same for us, and that the promise of God is enough for ourselves also, we start apologising for our trembling unbelief on the ground that our own case is of a peculiarly problematical nature. What stupidity is this!

Shall that which is made say to Him who made it: "Thou art not able to understand me or look after me"? Heart of mine, fling this wretched unbelief to the moles and the bats. Learn it once for all, and count it settled for evermore, that thine almighty Helper is equal to every challenge. Thy gravest extremity is His greatest opportunity. Remember His word, "I will never, *never* fail thee; and never, *never* forsake thee." Is even that not enough? Look up, and say it boldly, "The Lord is *my* helper: I will not fear." Well, says Frances Ridley Havergal:

> They who trust Him wholly
> Find him wholly true.

THE PURPOSE

Finally, observe the intended influence of this boldly affirmable fact in the experience of the believer. It is to be a

preservative against covetousness and fear. "Let your conversation be without covetousness, and be content with such
things as ye have, for He hath said . . .''

The wording here is intensely interesting. We need to
remember that three centuries have slipped away since our
Authorised Version first appeared, and words used in it have
undergone gradual modifications of meaning. This is true of
that word "conversation." Nowadays it is generally limited
to mean the speech of the lips; but when the Authorised Version was made the word meant one's whole manner of life.
Certainly the Greek word so translated here must not be
restricted to the speaking of the lips. It comes from a verb
meaning *to turn*; and in our text it means that our "turn of
mind," our mental attitude, our disposition, is to be *away
from* covetousness. Metaphorically, we are to have our backs
turned on this thing.

Look at the other words here. That expression, "without
covetousness" comes from a Greek negative meaning to be
free from the love of silver, or the love of money. The clause:
"Be content with such things as ye have," if we give the
Greek more literally, is "Be content with present things (or
present circumstances)." Thus the injunction runs:

"Let your turn of mind (your disposition) be free from the love
of money; and be content with your present circumstances."

There now, what say we to that? It is a straight, deep-
cutting sword-thrust to those in our churches who bow and
scrape to wealth or social position. It is a stinging rebuke to
those in our churches who play for position and prestige.
It is a smiting hand on the mouths of the unreasonable and
incessant grumblers among us. As with the impact of an
avalanche it sweeps away the wood, hay, stubble, on which
we have been standing. Men, money, circumstances—are
these the things to which the Christians or the churches must
look? Never! We are ever to say boldly, "The LORD is my
helper," because He has said, "I will never, never fail thee;
and never, never forsake thee."

Big terms these—"disposition," "money," "present circumstances." Why, these are the things which lie at the

very heart of the problem of life for men and women. A right attitude to money, a right adjustment to circumstances, a right attunement of disposition—these are the things which bring stable comfort to human hearts, build up strong, noble character, save men and women from crushing disappointments and life-souring embitterments; these are the things which light up the soul with the unclouded shinings of heaven.

Oh, that evil-eyed reptile, Covetousness! How it cuts its fangs into human hearts! How it fevers and poisons life with its venom! How its trail of slime makes ugly many an otherwise beautiful character! God save us from it! God save us from the love of money! The worship of the golden calf fills the earth with vanity and violence and vileness. God make us content with such things as we have, and with our present circumstances!

Mind you, being content with our present circumstances does not mean that we are to be supinely unconcerned about present evils which we can help to remedy, but it does mean that we are to be content with that personal position in life which a beneficent overruling Providence has seen proper for us; and it does mean also that we are to accept cheerfully those circumstances which are providentially permitted to surround us.

Nor does being content with our present circumstances mean a sluggard indifference to self-improvement. Nay, if we are truly content with what God has seen good for us we will by grateful endeavour turn it to the best account. Let us remember, however, that true self-improvement does not mean merely a rise in our salary, a higher position, a larger house, a swell car, but a greater love to God, a clearer perception of His will and ways, a truer likeness to the character of Christ, a more generous love to our brother, a truer fulfilling of just that place and purpose in this present life which God has had in His heart for us to fill. This is the real, the true, the only ultimately worthwhile self-improvement. Contentment is to take joyfully all that comes to us from God's hand, and to acquiesce trustingly in the will of God when things are taken from us.

The Hebrew Christians to whom the words of our text were addressed had undergone fierce persecutions in which their worldly goods had been confiscated. See how they are spoken of in the tenth chapter of this Hebrew epistle: "Ye endured

great afflictions." "Ye were made a gazingstock both by reproaches and afflictions." "Ye took joyfully the spoiling of your
goods, knowing in yourselves that ye have in heaven a better
and a more enduring substance." They had been plundered and
reduced. They had little or nothing left. Instead of glory they
had received contempt. Instead of raiment they had rags;
instead of silver, brass; instead of plenty, scarcity; instead of
houses, caves, holes, dens and the like. These are the people to
whom the words were first written: "Be content with your
present circumstances"! O how easily some of us give way to
bitter discontent! How we smart because we do not have the
possessions, the advantages, the successes, of another! How
seemingly incurably we forget that each one of us is inexpressibly
precious to Him Who redeemed us by His blood and tears, and
that He has said, "I will never, never fail *thee*; and never, never
forsake *thee*!"

We say it again, God save us from the love of money! The
British and American people are over-prone to it. And God
save us, His professing people, from *the fear of man!* The last
word in our text is against this crippling evil—"We may boldly
say: The Lord is my helper, and I will not fear what man shall
do unto me." The bread and wine of our communion table
recognize no essential difference between the millionaire and the
mill-worker. All men are but men. Our table also in its symbols
defies the utmost that men can do against us. What is the worst
that man can do against us? He can kill us, he can crucify us.
What then? Why this—says our communion table—the divine
Vindicator robs death of his prisoner. The Crucified rises: He
reigns; He returns; He rules; His crucifiers lick the dust, and the
nations bow before His feet! What fools we are to fear men
whose breath is in their nostrils, and who, after they have killed
the body, can do no more! Yet how this fear of man bringeth a
snare! How it paralyses many of us!

It is not always the fear of serious persecution which terrifies
us. Far oftener it is the fear of men's ridicule. Henry Martyn
was exposed both to peril and insult among the Moham-
medans in Persia, but he said that he found "sneers were more
difficult to bear than brickbats." This fear of ridicule hangs
about many a Christian like leaden chains. Sydney Smith truly
said, "You can no more exercise your reason, if you live in the

constant dread of laughter, than you can enjoy your life if you are in the constant terror of death." O that we might learn to say boldly, "The LORD is my helper: and I will not fear what man shall do unto me"! Neither sarcasm nor brutality can really harm us. In the presence of illness, adversity, persecution, danger, the true Christian can say with George Whitefield, "I am immortal till my work is done." Would that the challenge of the apostle might ever live before us as in letters of flame, "If God be for us, who can be against us?"

This fear of man expresses itself in a variety of ways. Let me catechize myself for a moment. Am I awkwardly self-conscious rather than Christ-conscious? Do I shrink from dislikeable duties and persons? Am I ready to endure hardness in business life rather than urge cowardly excuses of expediency? Do I always publicly side with Christ, no matter what company I may be in? Do I fear illness, poverty, loss, persecution, misunderstanding, ridicule, loneliness, adversity, death? The final part of our text is really in the form of a question, and should read thus (as it does in the later versions, and in Psalm cxviii from which it is a quotation)—"The Lord is my helper; I will not fear. *What shall man do unto me?*" When the words have this turn given to them they are the ringing challenge of a brave heart. This "what" covers everything that can possibly happen; and all that this "what" covers is itself covered by the promise of God—"I will never, never fail thee; and never, never forsake thee."

O fellow pilgrim to the celestial city, bind this strong, tender, enduring, all-sufficient Divine pledge to thy heart—"I will never, *never* fail thee; and never, *never* forsake thee." Then, with this flashing jewel bound to thy bosom, press onward, singing boldly—

> "The Lord is MY HELPER:
> I will not fear."

MY BELOVED

We see in burning-glasses, where the beams of the sun meet in one, how forcible they are, because there is a union of the beams in a little point. Let it be our labour that all the beams of our love may meet in Christ, that He may be our Beloved. As all streams meet in the great ocean, so let all our loves meet in Christ. We cannot bestow our love and our affections better than upon Christ. It is a happiness that we have such affections as joy, delight, and love, planted in us by God; and what a happiness is it that we should have such an excellent Object to fill those affections, yea, to transcend, and more than satisfy them!—RICHARD SIBBES.

O blessed conquest, to lose all things and to gain Christ! If I should tell you what I have found in Christ, ye or others could hardly believe me. Make Him your only, your Best-loved. Look into those depths of loveliness, sweetness, beauty, excellency, that are in Christ, and ye shall then cry down the whole world, and all the glory of it even when it is come to the summer-bloom.—

SAMUEL RUTHERFORD.

MY BELOVED

"My Beloved is mine, and I am His."—
Song of Sol. ii. 16.

"THERE is no book of Scripture on which more commentaries have been written and more diversities of opinion expressed than this short poem of eight chapters," writes a learned expositor. "It is acknowledged by those who are entirely disagreed as to its interpretation to possess features of extraordinary literary excellence, and to be not unworthy, as a composition, of the wise king whose name it bears." Internal evidences leave little room for doubt that the work is of the Solomonic period, and, indeed, that it actually came from the pen of the royal author to whom it is attributed.

But what shall we say about the *interpretation* of the book? We shall wisely guard against adding unprofitably to a voluminously discussed subject. Nor need we here make more than a few general comments, for in the process of time so much has been written around the question that certain broad facts now emerge with increasing clearness, all converging toward the same conclusion.

The canonicity of the book is unquestioned; and when we remember how the Hebrews venerated their sacred Scriptures, and how careful they were that only inspired writings should be included in the canon, this fact alone says a great deal. It is unbelievable that such a book should be given this decided place in the Jewish Scriptures, if merely of literary worth. Not one of the books is there simply as a piece of literature. Each has its place because of its religious character or its special connection with the peculiar national position of the Hebrew people. The very canonicity of the poem argues its spiritual significance.

Three theories of interpretation have been advanced, of which bare mention will here suffice. The *allegorical* theory ignores as of no concern whether the poem has any historical foundation in a real love suit between Solomon and Shulamith, and treats the whole as a purely figurative and mystical fiction. To read some of the absurd and fanciful expositions associated with this theory, such as that the hair of the bride represents the mass of the nations converted to Christianity, is too much for a God-given sense of humour, and brings the whole theory into disrepute.

At the other extreme is the *naturalistic* theory which wipes out any allegorical or even typical meaning, and regards the book simply as a collection of erotic songs, or idylls of love, put together simply on the ground of literary merit, though possibly intended to describe ideal human love. This theory leaves the inclusion of the book in the sacred canon an inexplicable anomaly.

Coming between these two is the *typical* interpretation, which recognizes the distinctive elements in each of the former views without going to the extreme of either. The poem has a historical basis, but in harmony with the rest of Scripture it also has a religious purpose and a spiritual content. An ideal human love is used to lead the soul into the thought of fellowship with God. Fundamentally the facts are historical, but they are lifted up into the region of poetry for a religious purpose; the facts are idealized, and given, by the Spirit of inspiration, a spiritual meaning.

We must not be deterred from a chastened perception of typical significances in Scripture because of the foolish extremes to which fanciful allegorizers have gone. Again and again in the Scriptures metaphors based upon the marriage relationship are applied to Israel's relationship with God, and to the Church's relationship with Christ, and to the individual soul's communion with God. The use of the marriage metaphor in connection with Christ and the Church is noticeably prominent in Paul and John; and we may well ask if they would thus have used the metaphor had not the Old Testament Scriptures already familiarised the people of God with the symbol. A true interpretation of the poem, therefore, will recognize in it a duality in unity; for while it is primarily the expression of "pure marital love as ordained of God in creation, and the vindication of that love as against both asceticism and lust," the deeper and larger meaning has reference to the heavenly Lover and His bride, the Church.

Thus, if the Song of Solomon spoke to Israel, it speaks in an even more profound and beautiful way to the spiritually quickened members of the true Church, concerning their relationship to the heavenly Bridegroom—of which relationship Paul was speaking when he wrote to the Ephesians, "Husbands love your wives, even as Christ also loved the Church, and gave Himself for it, that He might sanctify and cleanse it with the washing of water by the word, that He might present it to Himself a glorious Church, not having spot or wrinkle or any such thing, but that it should be holy and without blemish."

It has been well observed: "What so many of God's people (right down the course of the years) have recognised (in the Song of Solomon) must be substantially the mind of the Spirit." That the love of the Divine Bridegroom should "follow the analogies of the marriage relation seems evil only to minds so ascetic that marital desire itself seems to them unholy." The book has been a source of exquisite delight to the saintliest men and women of the ages. We see here, in hallowed type, the Lord Jesus and His mystic bride, the Church; and by a warrantable appropriation each believer may claim a true individual application.

What then is the climax of joy in this ideal espousal? It is the joy of mutual possession expressed in the words, "My Beloved is mine, and I am His"; and this is the quintessence of that holy joy which the believer finds in his wonderful union with the adorable Son of God, the assurance of possessing and being possessed. Let us therefore unhesitatingly take these words upon our lips as applying to ourselves and our dear Lord— "My Beloved is mine, and I am his."

What then are the bands which bind the saints and their Saviour together? What are the cords by which *He* is bound to *me*? And what are the cords by which *I* am bound to *Him*?

THE CORDS WHICH BIND HIM TO ME

First of all, He is bound to me by *the unbreakable cord of His promise.* "All that the Father giveth Me shall come to Me," He says, "and him that cometh to Me I will in no wise cast out." "He that believeth hath everlasting life, and shall not come into condemnation, but is passed from death unto life." "If any man hear My voice, and open the door, I will come in to him, and will sup with him, and he with Me." Of His believing people He says: "I give unto them eternal life, and they shall never perish, neither shall any man pluck them out of My hand." Ah, my soul, here is security indeed. Scattered through the sacred book there are doubtless scores of assurances given through prophets and apostles, but these now before thee are promises which fell from the lips of thine incarnate Lord Himself. He here gives Himself to us as our Shepherd, our Saviour, our Host, our Friend, our Life! His word is a cord which nought can break. "Firm as His throne His promise stands." His very character is bound up with His good word. Here is the assurance of faith. He is mine by His own promise which can never fail.

But He is also bound to me by *the unseverable cord of an eternal covenant.* "Christ loved the Church, and gave Himself for it." The word wings the mind away back through nineteen centuries to the green mound outside the city gate where the crucified Lord bowed His head in death. Nay, much more than that, the word reaches immeasurably farther back, even into the pre-historic ages. The Cross is not merely a happening in time. It has an eternal significance. What happened on Calvary did but express in terms of human history that which has been in the infinite Mind eternally. Before the mountains were brought forth, or ever God had made the earth, the Cross was there, in the counsels of Omniscience. That is why our blessed Lord is called "the Lamb slain from the foundation of the world." Yea, and the blood-bought Church was there too, for the word of inspiration tells us that the Church is "the mystery which from the beginning of the world hath been hid in God." There, away back through the ages, we find the Christ, the Cross, the Church. Read the words in their eternal setting: "Christ loved the Church, and gave Himself for it." How can we finite creatures of time grapple with the profundities of eternity? Yet we can adore where we can but dimly understand. From eternity Christ has loved the Church, and, by extension, every member in it. From eternity He has given Himself for us and to us, as our Saviour and our Divine Bridegroom. From eternity He has covenanted Himself to us, that we should be able to say for evermore, "My Beloved is mine, and I am His." Gaze on this mighty truth, O my soul. Is it indeed true that before the first sunrise gilded

Eden's delectable paradise with glory, and before the first father of the race had opened his eyes to admire that scene of unmatched loveliness, the Son of God had covenanted Himself to me? How then can I but be lost in wonder, love, and praise? How can I but love Him with all my heart and mind and soul and strength? How can I allow anything in my life which would grieve or dishonour my glorious divine Lover who has loved me eternally and sealed His love in the blood of Calvary?

But again, my Beloved is bound to me by the _golden cord of Divine love_. O the love of Christ for us! How amazing it is! We have already touched upon it in speaking of the eternal covenant by which He has bound himself to us; but what shall we say in the presence of Calvary? Thought reels back overwhelmed. "The Son of God loved me, and gave Himself for me." O mystery of mysteries, wonder of wonders, that HE should thus love _me_! He "_gave Himself_" for me. Who shall tell the immensity and intensity in that word? My heart trembles with strange emotion to read it. He bore the scourge, the nails, the thorns, the spear-gash, the shame, the agony, for _me_! O the love of my dear Lord! Who shall tell it? Who shall measure the measureless? Who shall declare the dimensions of that which is infinite? Who shall gauge the depth of anguish through which He plunged to win the love of my poor soul, and to make me His own? Who shall sound His praise? Come, ye denizens of the heavenly Zion, lend me celestial eloquence that I may rise above the stammering syllables of this earth-bound tongue. "My Beloved is mine!" In the consummate miracle of that uttermost sacrifice on Calvary He has once for all given Himself for me and to me. O how then shall I dare keep back anything from _Him_? How shall I dare to say, "My Beloved is mine" without adoringly adding "and I am His"?

> How can I, Lord, withhold
>   Life's brightest hour
> From Thee, or gathered gold,
>   Or any power?
> Why should I keep one precious thing from Thee?
> When Thou hast giv'n Thine own dear Self for me?

Yet again, "My Beloved is mine," bound to me by _the proven cord of experience_. Do I not know that He is mine from the way in which He has revealed Himself to me? The eyes of millions are closed to His loveliness; yet in the mystery of His love he has touched these eyes, these inward heart-eyes of mine, by His quickening Spirit, that I might behold His beauty, and see Him to be "the chiefest among ten thousand," yea the "altogether lovely." Do I not know that He is mine as I recall the hours of rapturous fellowship with Him in the place of prayer? Ah, sweet thought, how real He has made Himself! How the moments have sped away unnoticed in those blest seasons! How the place of communion has at times seemed transported into the heavenly realms! My soul, thou canst not forget these manifestations of thy Lord. The fragrance of His garments still lingers with thee. Heaven was nearer than earth, and Jesus more real than any other presence in the universe. Do I not know that He is mine by the way He has made Himself real and satisfying to me through all the changeful experiences of my days? Glory to Thy Name, dear Lord, Thou hast not left me in doubt about this glorious fact. Thou hast given Thine own Spirit to indwell my heart, constantly witnessing that Thou art mine; and truly Thy love, what it is, none but Thy loved ones know.

> Lord, Thou hast made Thyself to me
> 　A living, bright reality;
> More present, to faith's vision keen,
> 　Than any earthly object seen;
> More dear, more intimately nigh,
> Than e'en the closest human tie.

THE CORDS WHICH BIND ME TO HIM

And now what are the cords by which *I* am bound to *Him*? First, I am bound to Him by *the old cord of creation*, that is, I belong to Him by His right of ownership as my Creator, and because of my creaturely dependence upon Him. Let me ever bear this in mind. I am in no sense the independent proprietor of my own being. I am His property. All that I have He gave me. All that I am He made me—all except the disfigurement due to sin, both hereditary and self-committed. In Him I "live and move and have my being." This primary Creator-creature cord which binds me to "my Beloved" has become unspeakably precious, for it binds me to One who has revealed Himself as a "faithful

Creator"; and unless *this* cord had first been wound around me, none of the other bands which make me His would have encircled me. It is our very Creator who has become united to us in spiritual wedlock. Even as He saith through His prophet, "Thy *Maker* is thine *husband*"!

Second, I am bound to Him by *the red cord of redemption*. O prodigy of grace, that He who made me by His power should redeem me by His blood! "Ye are bought with a price," He says to His people. Yea, what a price! Moved with wonder that the incarnate Son of God should undergo such agonies as those of Gethsemane and Gabbatha and Golgotha, the poet exclaims, "A thousand worlds so þought were bought too dear." Angels look on in amazement as the ransom price is paid in the dread drops of that blood and agony. O the love that sought me! O the blood that bought me!

> And what is this? Survey the wondrous cure;
> And at each step let higher wonder rise!
> Pardon for infinite offence! and pardon
> Through means that speak its value infinite!
> A pardon bought with blood, with blood divine!
> With blood divine of Him I made my foe!
> Persisted to provoke, though woo'd and awed
> Bless'd and chastised, a flagrant rebel still!
> A rebel, midst the thunders of His throne!
> Nor I alone, a rebel, universe!
> My species up in arms, not one exempt!
> Yet for the foulest of the foul He dies,
> Most joyed for the redeemed from deepest guilt,
> As if our race were held of highest rank,
> And Godhead dearer as more kind to man!
> Leap, every heart! and every bosom, burn!
> O what a scale of miracles is here!
> Its lowest round high planted on the skies,
> Its towering summit lost beyond the thought
>   of man or angel!

O the grace and glory of this redemption! Not with silver or gold have I been redeemed, nor with the most resplendent material possessions in the infinite treasuries of the Godhead. Such is my guilt and bondage, such my exposure to eternal ruin, and such my relationship toward God, that to redeem me He must needs give *Himself*. "God was in Christ." In Christ He suffered to redeem me. Well may the blood of Jesus be called "precious blood"! Well may our heavenly Bridegroom say to each of His dearly purchased people, "I have redeemed thee: thou art Mine"!

Again, I am bound to Him by *the strong cord of election*. My conversion to Christ was not the chance product of fortuitous circumstances. Nay, my regeneration by the Spirit of God is itself the evidence of a predetermining Divine purpose. The subject of Divine election may indeed be more than a little enshrouded in mystery, but this in no measure detracts from its reality. If the Divine choice of a peculiar people, in Christ, from the eternal ages, be not a fact, then those Scriptures which we have learned to look upon as the oracles of God are no more than a fabrication of human ideas and conceits. We know the book too well to entertain such a thought for one moment. Election in Christ is one of the most glorious verities unveiled to us in the Scripture revelation; and it is one of the believer's most comforting securities. Who shall gainsay such words as the following?

"He hath chosen us in Him before the foundation of the world, that we should be holy and without blame before Him in love; having predestinated us unto the adoption of children by Jesus Christ unto Himself, according to the good pleasure of His will; that in the ages to come He might show the exceeding riches of His grace in His kindness toward us through Christ Jesus."— Eph. i. 4–5, and ii. 7.

"Moreover, whom He did predestinate, them He also called; and whom He called, them He also justified; and whom He justified, them He also glorified."—Rom. viii. 30.

O the mystery, the majesty, the mercy of it! To the believer there is no sweeter expression in Scripture than this—"The election of grace," for it speaks at one and the same time the Divine sovereignty and the Divine love, which together in one bind us forever to the heart of the Lord Jesus. Ah, this is a strong cord indeed. If God chose me in Christ away back in pre-terrestrial ages I have security for ever. He will never give me up, and never let me go.

Once more, I am bound to Him by *the new cord of my own choice*. My heavenly Prince has ridden forth in resistless conquest to make my heart His captive. Vain was the struggle against His glorious love. At length my heart, subdued, sank down at His nail-scarred feet, exclaiming:

> I yield, I yield,
>   I can hold out no more;
> I sink, by dying love compelled,
>   And own Thee Conqueror!

O the blessedness of that moment! O the bliss of this willing bondage! He has completely captivated me. His gentleness hath made Him great. In eager submission and glad self surrender I have given myself now to Him for time and eternity. Oh, that this rebellious and stubborn heart should have contended so long and blindly against my matchless royal Lover! But now, all is different. As thoughtfully as eagerly, and as completely as irrevocably, I have chosen Him as mine, and have given myself to Him while life itself shall endure.

These, then, are the cords which bind my Lord and me together, so that I can now say, from a grateful and adoring heart, "My Beloved is mine, and I am His." All but one of these cords are those which He Himself has thrown around me and securely tied; and even the exceptional one must be attributed to the gentle, persistent pressure of His Spirit within my heart. What cords, what bands, are these! They can never decay with age; and none can ever sunder them.

> I've found a Friend, O such a Friend,
>   He loved me ere I knew Him;
> He drew me with the cords of love,
>   And thus He bound me to Him.
> And round my heart still closely twine
>   Those cords which naught can sever;
> For I am His, and He is mine,
>   For ever and for ever.

THE CHARACTERISTICS OF THIS UNION

Let us now briefly note some of the more outstanding characteristics of this wonderful union, as indicated in the words of the bride. Observe at once that it is a *present* union—"my Beloved *is* mine, and I *am* His." This was the first element in the rapture of fair Shulamith; and this is also the first of those "live coals" which feed the flame of joy in the heart of the Christian. Jesus is mine as a present possession. The public declaration of our union may yet be future, at "the Marriage

Supper of the Lamb"; but even now He is truly mine, as saith the apostle, "He that is joined to the Lord is (even now) one spirit."

Then, also, this union, besides being present, is *certain*. There is neither presumption with its forwardness, nor doubt with its backwardness, in the bride's word. There is not a suggestion of indefiniteness. The mutual possession is affirmed with the unfaltering voice of perfect assurance. He "*is*" mine. I "*am*" His. It is even so with the believer and his Lord. We are not left to the mercy of "peradventures" and "perhapses." Each of the Spirit-born can say "I *know* whom I have believed." As saith the apostle, "Ye have an unction from the Holy One, and ye *know*." Thank God, we *know*! We know that He abideth in us; and the Spirit of God has put the song of the redeemed within us—"Christ in you, the hope of glory."

It goes almost without saying that the union in which the bride here exults is supremely *joyous*. What exhilaration breathes through the glad cry, "My Beloved is mine, and I am His"! All too often has wedlock been iron fetters instead of silken bands. Instead of bringing supernal joys it has dragged infernal miseries with it. Sin has blasted the coveted paradise, and made the marriage contract a cord of thorns. But where pure love lifts its sceptre the nuptial pledge brings something of the joy of heaven itself to bide on earth. O the joy where true love sets two hearts beating as one! It was thus with the ideal love of the royal lover and his spouse of long ago: and it is thus with the believer and his Lord to-day. Joy of all joys, to know that "my Beloved is mine and I am His"! What are the worldling's fancied pleasures but bursting bubbles and deceits of the imagination when compared with *this* spiritual bliss?

> O this is life! O this is joy!
> My God, to find Thee so!

Following immediately upon this is the basic fact that this union is a *loving* union. Who can find words to describe the love-bond between the redeemed and the Redeemer? Language breaks down here. As for *His* love to us, we know not which is the greater, the mystery or the reality of it. As for *our* love to *Him*, while in the first place we love Him *gratefully*, for what He has done for us, we have learned now to love Him *adoringly*, for what He is in Himself; yea, we have come to love Him in a way which we can only struggle to describe as *absorbingly*—we feel that our very life goes out to Him with our love, while His own love brings *His* very life into our hearts.

> O love Divine, how sweet Thou art!
> When shall I find my willing heart
>   All taken up by Thee?
> I thirst, I faint, I die to prove
>   The fulness of redeeming love,—
>   The love of Christ to me.

"My Beloved is mine, and I am His"—this is a *complete* union. The bridegroom and the bride have given themselves fully to each other. Christ has given Himself fully to His mystic bride. Christ is mine in all His offices and capacities—in His incarnation, in His teaching, in His redeeming, in His resurrection life, in His exaltation, in His second advent and the glory of His coming reign, yea, and in all the blessedness of His eternal glory! He is altogether *mine*. O the wonder of it! My heart, what of thy present response to all this? Truly thou art Christ's by unmistakable bonds; but hast thou completed *thy* part by giving thyself up entirely to Him here and now?

"My Beloved is mine, and I am His"—this is a *complex* union. Shulamith's beloved is Israel's sovereign. To be *His* bride is to sustain a variety of relationships. So is it with the believer and his royal Lord. It takes a complexity of metaphors to express such a unique union. Christ is the head and we are the body—for it is a *living* union. Christ is the bridegroom and we are the bride—for it is a *loving* union. Christ is the foundation and we are the building—for it is a *lasting* union. Christ is the vine and we are the branches—for it is a *fruitful* union. Christ is the Firstborn and we are His brethren—for it is a union of joint-heirship. But we must forbear. There is no more wonderful study in Scripture than that of our complex union with the Son of God.

"My Beloved is mine"—that word "mine," does it not speak the fact that Jesus belongs to His people *individually*? He is not just *ours*. He is *mine*. I may have Him as though there were none other in heaven or on earth beside me. Again, when the bride says, "My Beloved is mine," is she not speaking out of a real *experience* of what she affirms? And cannot I, too, say that Jesus is mine by conscious, personal experience, by the indwelling of His Spirit within my heart? O how much more remains to be said about this exclamation of Solomon's typical bride which we cannot stay to say here! We cannot resist a further glance at that possessive pronoun, however— "My Beloved." Like a bee which comes back again and again to the same flower, we find our eyes turning back again and again to that word. O the unutterable sense of blessedness which fills the heart when we take that word upon our lips! "MY Beloved is MINE"—what a world in a word!

> I know He's mine, that Friend so dear;
> He lives with me; He's ever near.
> Ten thousand charms around Him shine;
> But best of all, I know He's MINE!

We must mention one further characteristic of our union with Christ, namely, that it is *indissoluble*. Could but the thought that our saving and glorifying oneness with Him might ever be dissolved gain a hold upon us, that ghastly thought would quite unparadise the realms of light; but we know that nought shall ever put us assunder. Hear again the word of Scripture: "Who shall separate us from the love of Christ? Neither death nor life nor angels nor principalities nor powers nor things present nor things to come nor height nor depth nor any other thing created shall be able to separate us from the love of God which is in Christ Jesus our Lord."

> From Him who loves me now so well
> What power my soul shall sever?
> Shall life or death or earth or hell?
> No, I am His for ever!

THE CONSEQUENCES OF THIS UNION

There is much we should like to have said about the *results* of all this in the present experience of the believer, but we can make only two or three observations in closing.

Come, child of God, can you not "amen" the fact that this wondrous relationship with the Lord Jesus pervades the heart with a serene *tranquillity*? Though poverty should beset me, though all my worldly goods should be confiscated, yet if "my

Beloved is mine and I am His" I am boundlessly rich. Though adversity reduce me, and troubles assail me, in this will I be confident while I can say, "My Beloved is mine and I am His." The things which once perturbed and distracted my soul have lost their power to affright me since I entered into the realization that "My Beloved is mine and I am His." The Lord help us *all* into the harbour of this blessed rest!

> Things that once were wild alarms
>   Cannot now disturb my rest;
> Closed in everlasting arms,
>   Pillowed on His loving breast.
> Oh to lie for ever here,
>   Doubt and care and self resign,
> While He whispers in my ear
>   I am His, and He is mine!

But besides this, dear Christian believer, is it not true that the more we delight to say, "My Beloved is mine, and I am His," so the more do our hearts become possessed by a determined *resolution* to speak abroad the excellences of our incomparable Beloved? Where is His like among the sons of earth? The hills and valleys may pass the echo round, yet never shall there come forth a Prince and a Saviour such as He. "There is none other name under heaven given among men whereby we must be saved." O this almighty, all-gracious, all-glorious Shepherd, Saviour, Satisfier, Sovereign! As the old-time Shulamite maiden spake of *her* beloved to the daughters of Jerusalem and the men of the city, must we not speak forth "the praises of Him who hath called us out of darkness into His marvellous light?" May our love loose our lips, for surely silence is sin!

Finally, our consciousness of this wonderful oneness with Christ fills us with eager *anticipation*. We long for His appearing even as Shulamith longed for the return of her kingly lover. As soon as she has said, "My beloved is mine, and I am his," she continues, "Until the day break, and the shadows flee away, turn, my beloved, and be thou like a roe or a young hart upon the mountains of Bether." So is it with the true lover of Jesus. How can he say, "My Beloved is mine, and I am His," without adding, "Even so, come, Lord Jesus"? There is no doctrine in all the Scriptures more precious than that of the

Lord's second advent. O for *that* daybreak, when the shadows
shall flee away for ever, and we shall "see Him as He is" and be
"like Him"! Then will our song be that of Solomon's Shulamite
—"Lo, the winter is past, the rain is over and gone; the flowers
appear on the earth; the time of the singing of birds is come,
and the voice of the turtle is heard in our land." "Even so,
come, Lord Jesus!"

> His for ever, only His;
>   Who the Lord and me shall part?
> Ah, with what a rest of bliss
>   Christ can fill the loving heart!
> Heaven and earth may fade and flee,
>   First-born light in gloom decline;
> But while God and I shall be,
>   I am His, and He is mine.

MY LORD

This soul of ours hath love, and cannot but love some fair one; and O what a fair One, what an only One, what an excellent, lovely, ravishing One, is Jesus! O come all, and drink at this living well. Come, drink, and live for evermore. Come, drink, and welcome; welcome saith our fairest Bridegroom. No man getteth Christ with ill-will: no man cometh and is not welcome: no man cometh and rueth his voyage. All men speak well of Christ who have been at Him.—SAMUEL RUTHERFORD.

> Higher than the highest heaven,
> Deeper than the deepest sea,
> Lord, Thy love at last hath conquered;
> Grant me now my soul's desire,—
> None of self, and all of Thee!—
>
> THEODORE MONOD.

MY LORD

"The excellency of the knowledge of Christ Jesus my Lord."
Phil. iii. 8.

IN PHILIPPIANS iii. 7–10, Paul writes, "But what things were gain to me, those I counted loss for Christ. Yea doubtless, and I count all things but loss for the excellency of the knowledge of Christ Jesus my Lord: for whom I have suffered the loss of all things, and do count them but refuse, that I may win Christ, and be found in Him, not having mine own righteousness which is of the law, but that which is through the faith of Christ, the righteousness which is of God by faith: that I may know Him, and the power of His resurrection, and the fellowship of his sufferings, being made conformable unto His death."

These are fervent and glorious words. They are the overflow of a heart full beyond containing with love to Christ. The reservoir brims over and finds relief in a glad outpouring. It has been truly said that Christian service can be either overwork or overflow. If it is overwork it means nerve-strain and eventual weariness; but if it be the overflow from an inward replenishment there is ease and freshness and gladness about it. It is ever the overflow of heart that gives a man the tongue of true eloquence and the pen of a ready writer. When our prayer life is regular and real, and our communion with Christ rich and deep, there is a quality about our service, and a restfulness in it, which come from the communicated fulness of Christ Himself.

"Christ Jesus *my* Lord"—note the pronoun. Paul is giving a personal testimony. This is the one place in Paul's writings where we have the expression, "Christ Jesus *my* Lord." How remarkable is this pronoun "my" here, when we consider by whom it is used! This is none other than Saul of Tarsus, the one-time ringleader of the anti-Nazarene persecutors, the raging Pharisee who made havoc among the early Christians, and cursed the name of Jesus before rulers and people. Behold, a miracle of transforming grace has happened!

See with what noble passion he now expresses himself. Christ Jesus is truly his "*Lord*." He is everything to him. "What things were gain to me, those I counted loss for Christ. Yea doubtless, and I count all things but loss for the excellency of the knowledge of Christ Jesus my Lord, for whom I have suffered the loss of all things, and do count them refuse, that I may win Christ." Jesus Himself is Paul's (and our) super-abounding compensation for every renunciation.

Dr. A. T. Pierson holds that the passage in which these words occur is the key to the whole epistle. Philippians, he says, is the disciple's *balance-sheet*, and the key word is "gain." Here in Paul's personal testimony the thought of loss and gain finds concentration, though the Authorised Version some-what obscures this. In verse 8, where Paul is translated as saying "that I may win Christ," the awkward word "win" should be "gain," as in other places where the same Greek word occurs; and in verse 7 the word "gain" should be plural; so that the passage reads—

"What things were GAINS to me, those I counted LOSS for Christ. Yea, verily, and I count all things to be LOSS for the excellency of the knowledge of Christ Jesus my Lord, for whom I have suffered the LOSS of all things, and do count them refuse that I may GAIN Christ, and be found in Him."

What were the gains which Paul counted loss for Christ? In verses 4, 5, 6, he lists the things which he renounced at his conversion. They were things which must have meant more to a zealous Jew than we to-day can easily realise. "If any other man thinketh that he hath whereof he might glory in the flesh, I more," he says.

1. "*Circumcised the eighth day*." Paul was no mere proselyte, but an Israelite by birth, having, by heredity and the sign of the covenant, his part in the covenant promises of Israel; and like many another, he was proud of this.

2. "*Of the stock of Israel*." Paul's parents, also, were not merely proselytes, but were themselves Hebrews by

birth. Paul was of Israelite descent through and through; and he was proud of his unblemished pedigree.

3. *"Of the tribe of Benjamin."* The tribe which gave the first king to Israel; which remained true to the Davidic throne when the other tribes broke away; which had helped Judah and Levi to restore the temple; and within the boundary of which stood the Holy City.

4. *"An Hebrew of the Hebrews."* Although living at Tarsus, Paul's parents adhered to the Hebrew language and customs. Paul was no Hellenist by upbringing, but was educated at Jerusalem under the famous Gamaliel. He was proficient in the Hebrew language and Scriptures, and adhered to Hebrew customs.

5. *"As touching the law, a Pharisee."* By birth an Israelite, by upbringing a Hebrew, he was also, by his own choice, a Pharisee. He had embraced the straitest sect—the one which took the strictest view of the law.

6. *"Concerning zeal, persecuting the church."* Paul was not satisfied even with being a Pharisee. He was a *zealous* Pharisee, the conscientious and relentless persecutor of all heretics and heretical sects.

7. *"Touching the righteousness which is in the law, blameless."* So far as the observance of all the formal rules, precepts, and practices of the law were concerned, Paul measured up to the last requirement.

In outward grounds of confidence no man could surpass Paul. Yet all confidence in these things, and any supposed merit accruing from them, had been once for all thrown overboard when his suddenly floundering vessel had struggled through troubled waters to its new haven in the encircling arms of the risen Christ Jesus; and now he writes, "What things were gains to me, these I counted loss for Christ."

These things, however, are far from being the only things which Paul gives up for His Lord's sake. His renunciation increases as time goes on, until now, as he writes to the Philippians, he says, "I count ALL things but loss for Christ Jesus my Lord." Nor is Paul's sweeping abandonment anything of a merely theoretical nature, for he adds *"I have suffered* the loss of all things."

Thus Paul puts down loss after loss on the one side, while on the other there is but one item—"CHRIST JESUS MY LORD." How much Paul has given up for his Lord! He has parted with the things dear to him as life itself. But now he has found more than all he has lost, and he thrills to know that having given up so much, he is more fully Christ's, and Christ is the more fully his own. We begin to realise what intensity of affection there is in that possessive pronoun, "Christ Jesus MY Lord."

"Christ Jesus MY Lord." Those who give up most for Jesus love Him most dearly, and possess Him most satisfyingly. Perhaps He would mean more to some of ourselves if we gave up more for Him. Some of us are in business. For whom do we make money—for ourselves or *Him*? All of us have time to dispose of. How do we use it—for ourselves or *Him*? How much or how little does our professed love for Jesus express itself in sacrifice?

But now let us go further. Paul, having counted all things loss for the "excellency of the knowledge of Christ Jesus my Lord," finds the supreme passion of his heart to be that he might know his Lord more and more. Look again at that tenth verse: "That I may know Him, and the power of His resurrection, and the fellowship of His sufferings, being made conformable unto His death." Paul desires to know Christ in a threefold way: (i) Christ Himself, (ii) the power of His resurrection, (iii) the fellowship of His sufferings. We find a remarkable and instructive parallel with this in the eleventh and twelfth chapters of John, in the account of Martha and Mary and Lazarus. Of Martha we may truly say that she knew *"Him."* Of Lazarus we may say that he knew "the power of His resurrection." Of Mary we may say that she knew something of "the fellowship of His sufferings." Turn back to John xi and xii, and see how truly this is so.

The emphatic thing about Martha is that while she expressed perplexity about her brother's death, and about the delay of Jesus to come when sent for, she could say most clearly and definitely concerning the person of Christ Himself, "I know." Observe her use of that expression: "I know." In verses 21 and 22 we read, "Then said Martha unto Jesus: Lord, if Thou hadst been here my brother had not died; but I KNOW that even now, whatsoever Thou wilt ask of God, God will give it Thee." Then in verses 23 and 24 we read, "Jesus saith unto her: Thy brother shall rise again. Martha saith unto Him: I KNOW that he shall rise again in the resurrection at the last day." Following this, we find that the Lord utters a striking challenge to Martha, and receives a remarkable reply. "Jesus saith unto her; I am the resurrection and the life; he that believeth in Me, though he were dead, yet shall he live; and whosoever liveth and believeth in Me shall never die. *Believest thou this?*" In reply to this challenge Martha says: "Yea Lord; I believe that *Thou art the Christ the Son of God, which should come into the world.*" Truly Martha could say "I know HIM!"

Lazarus could say that he knew something of "the power of His resurrection." The Lord Jesus demonstrated that he had resurrection power within Himself before His own resurrection took place. He showed it in the raising of Lazarus. There are seven outstanding facts in the account concerning Lazarus. We see him—

1. Dead—"Then said Jesus unto them plainly: Lazarus is dead" (xi. 14).

2. Raised—"He that was dead came forth" (xi. 44), "Lazarus . . . raised from the dead" (xii. 9).

3. Bound—"He that was dead came forth, bound hand and foot" (xi. 44).

4. Loosed—"Jesus saith unto them: Loose him, and let him go" (xi. 44).

5. Feasting—"Lazarus was one of them that sat at the table with Him" (xii. 2).

6. Witnessing—"Much people came that they might see Lazarus whom He had raised" (xii. 9).

7. Convincing—"By reason of him many of the Jews believed on Jesus" (xii. 11).

Thus we may say that illustratively Lazarus knew the power of Christ's resurrection in new life, in liberation, in communion, and in service.

As for Mary, *she* knew something of "the fellowship of His sufferings." Three times in the Gospel records we come across Mary, and each time she is at the Master's feet. The first time we see her is in Luke x. 38, 39. "It came to pass, as they went, that He entered into a certain village, and a certain woman named Martha received Him into her house. And she had a sister called Mary, which also sat *at Jesus' feet* and heard (was listening to) His word."' Next, in John xi we see her mourning her brother's death, and she carries her grief to the feet of Jesus. "She fell down *at His feet*, saying: Lord if Thou hadst been here my brother had not died." The third time we see her is in John xii. Six days before the crucifixion she breaks the alabastron adoringly at His feet. "Then took Mary a pound of ointment of spikenard, very costly, and *anointed the feet of Jesus*, and wiped His feet with her hair; and the house was filled with the odour of the ointment." From these three glimpses of Mary we see that—

She sat at His feet to *learn* (Luke x. 39).

She took to His feet her *grief* (John xi. 32).

She gave at His feet her *best* (John xii. 3).

Here in this twelfth chapter of John, where we see Mary bending with her costly gift at the Lord's feet, we have an exquisite picture of consecration to Christ. There are five prominent figures in the story: Martha, Lazarus, Mary, Judas, and the Lord Jesus; and all five have a clearly representative significance. Martha stands for service; Lazarus for communion; Mary for consecration; Judas for the world's attitude to consecration; while the Lord Jesus represents the *divine* attitude. Look at the chapter again, and see how unmistakable all this is.

Martha—*Service*. "Jesus, six days before the Passover, came to Bethany. There they made Him a supper; and Martha served."

Lazarus—*Communion.* "But Lazarus was one of them that sat at the table with Him."

Mary—*Consecration.* "Then took Mary a pound of ointment of spikenard, very costly, and anointed the feet of Jesus, and wiped His feet with her hair; and the house was filled with the odour of the ointment."

Judas—*The world's attitude.* "Then saith Judas: Why was not this ointment sold for three hundred pence and given to the poor? This he said not that he cared for the poor, but because he was a thief, and had the bag, and bare what was put therein."

Jesus—*The divine attitude.* "Then said Jesus: Let her alone; against the day of My burying hath she kept this. For the poor always ye have with you, but Me ye have not always." ("She hath wrought a good work on Me." "Verily I say unto you: Wheresoever this Gospel shall be preached in the whole world, there shall also this that this woman hath done be told for a memorial of her."—Matt. xxvi, 10 and 13.)

But the most significant thing of all is Christ's explanation of *Mary's motive and insight.* He says, "Against the day of My burying hath she kept this." "In that she hath poured this ointment on My body, she did it for My burial." Again and again in the later months of His ministry the Lord had spoken of His coming sufferings and death, but the disciples had been slow of heart to understand or to believe. Peter, speaking for the rest, had said, "Be it far from Thee, Lord, this shall not be unto Thee"; and the Lord had uttered the strange rejoinder, "Get thee behind Me, Satan; thou art an offence unto Me; for thou savourest not the things that be of God, but those that be of men." The disciples did not understand. Yet among the followers of Jesus there was one, a woman, who had grasped the true significance of His words and the supreme purpose of His coming into the world. It was Mary of Bethany, the woman who sat at the feet of Jesus. She had learned the inner truth, the deeper, bigger, grander thing. When all others failed to grasp the real issue, she understood! —and she came to anoint the world's Saviour in anticipation of His sacrificial death.

What understanding and sympathy, then, leaked forth with Mary's outpoured anointing oil! What must it have meant to the heart of Him who, besides being God indeed, was truly man! Mary was sharing His sufferings with Him! Truly, if Martha knew *"Him,"* and Lazarus knew "the power of His *resurrection,"* Mary had entered into "the fellowship of His *sufferings."*

"That I may know Him, and the power of His resurrection, and the fellowship of His sufferings, being made conformable unto His death." The supreme passion of the Christian heart should be to know Christ—to know *"Him,"* personally and intimately, to know Him experientially in "the power of His resurrection," to know Him in that deepest and closest of all ways, in the oneness of a sympathetic, heart-to-heart fellowship in His sufferings over a world with its back turned on God.

But I can only know Him thus when I make Him truly "MY LORD," counting all things loss for His dear sake, living wholly for Him, and keeping daily tryst with Him in the quiet place. This is open to all of us, even though we must give hours of each day to mundane things; and who shall tell the rich, deep, spiritual joys which come to those who know the Lord Jesus thus?

I sometimes fear that, despite all our busy Christian service, our attending meetings and conventions, our singing of hymns, and all our outward Christian activities, some of us, even though we are truly trusting on the finished work of Calvary for our salvation, may find, when we pass beyond, that we do not know *Jesus Himself,* having so neglected the secret tryst with Christ down here that we find ourselves strangers to Him there.

On one occasion when the late King George the Fifth was staying at Holyrood Palace, Edinburgh, groups of people were lingering on a pathway overlooking the palace grounds, in the hope of catching a glimpse of his Majesty as he came out to the palace grounds. One of these waiting groups consisted of four women who were busily talking to each other about the worthy king. Two of them said they had seen him several times and knew him well by sight. They were rather proud to have this advantage over the other two women who had never seen him. Oh, yes, they knew the king well enough, and would tell the other two women when he walked into the palace grounds. After a time, the tall, lithe figure of a military-looking gentleman strode into the palace grounds. "There he is! There's the king!" exclaimed the two women to their friends. A person who stood nearby, however, quietly corrected them. "No, that is not the king. That is a military officer." Almost immediately afterward the king himself, a much smaller figure, walked into the grounds. "See, *there* is the king," said the person who had corrected them. The two women who had professed to know the king so well were filled with embarrassment to realise that they had made such a mistake after speaking so confidently. They had professed to know the king, but they did not really know him at all; and when the king came forth they did not recognize him! Are some of ourselves like those two women? My heart, may it not be so with thee!

"That I may know Him"—are some of us so full of ourselves and our busy servings that we cannot see Christ in all His beauty? Some years ago, when I was away on a preaching appointment, my wife and little daughter stayed at the home of a friend. On the bedroom wall, just over the head of the bed in which they slept, there was a picture of the Lord Jesus, which was reflected in the large mirror of the dressing-table standing in the bay of the bedroom window. When my little daughter woke on her first morning there, she saw the picture reflected in the mirror while she still lay in bed, and exclaimed, "Oh, mommy, I can see Jesus through the mirror!" Then she quickly kneeled up to take a better look, but in so doing brought her own body between the picture and the mirror, so that instead of seeing the picture of Jesus reflected she now saw herself. So she lay down again, and again saw the picture of Jesus. She was up and down several times after that, with her eye fixed on the mirror. Then she said, "Mommy, when I can't see myself I can see Jesus; but every time I see myself I don't see Him." How true it is that when self fills the vision we do not see Jesus!

This is the trouble with many of us. We block our own vision of Him. We are in the way of our own eye. We must first get ourselves away from obstructing the soul's gaze. We must get to where Paul was when he said, "I count all things loss for the excellency of the knowledge of Christ Jesus my Lord."

It is thus that He truly becomes "MY LORD." It is thus that with clearer eyes we come to behold His incomparable loveliness. It is thus that with purer hearts we come to know His joy and peace and power and love and abiding presence. It is thus that we become growingly like Him, being conformed to His own beauteous image.

One of the things which modern psychology has definitely demonstrated is what we call *intergrade*. There is a marked tendency for mutual assimilation between persons who love each other, who are continually in each other's presence, and under each other's influence. A photographic society in Geneva, we are told, has taken photographs of seventy-eight married couples, and of an equal number of adult brothers and sisters. On careful inspection it has been found that the married couples show more likeness between the one member and the other than do brother and sister of the same blood to each other. Have we not all seen happily married couples who have shared life together through many years exhibiting this assimilation, this mutual approximation, this intergrade? There has gradually developed a perfect understanding between the one mind and the other, a blending of interests, a similar way of looking at things. Such intergrade can be a beautiful thing. And should not the Christian reveal something like this in the gradual approximation of his character to that of His Lord? Should not the beauty of that matchless One escape through these lives of ours?

There is a beautiful prayer comes down to us from St. Richard of Chichester, a saint of the thirteenth century, a prayer which, God grant, we may make our own—

> Day by day, dear Lord,
> Of Thee three things I pray:
> To see Thee more clearly,
> Love Thee more dearly,
> Follow Thee more nearly,
> Day by day.

MY GOD

If God be thy portion, there is no condition that can make thee miserable: if God be not thy portion, there is no condition that can make thee happy. If God be not thy portion, in the midst of thy sufficiency thou wilt be in straits. O sirs, it is not absolutely necessary that you should have this or that earthly portion, but it is absolutely necessary that you should have God.—THOMAS BROOKS.

> The rich man in his wealth confides,
> But in my God my trust abides.
>   Laugh as ye will, I hold
> This one thing fast that He hath taught:
> Who trusts in God shall want for naught.
>
> Yes, Lord, Thou art as rich to-day
> As Thou hast been, and shalt be aye;
>   I rest on Thee alone.
> Thy riches to my soul be given,—
> And 'tis enough for earth and heaven!
>   —HANS SACHS.

MY GOD

"But my God shall supply all your need according to His riches
n glory by Christ Jesus."—Phil. iv. 19.

C. H. SPURGEON, in one of his printed sermons, says he constantly feared lest amid much preaching he should fall into
preaching *about* the Gospel rather than preaching the Gospel
itself. To counteract this danger he was wont to preach
periodically from some well-known Gospel text about which
he felt it was practically impossible to say anything new;
thus compelling himself to declare the plain truths of the
Gospel without the slightest attempt at novelty or brilliance.
This is a noble example which many a preacher to-day would
do well to follow!

Now the verse which we are here considering is one of the
best known and best loved in the Bible. It has been blessed
to more hearts than could be counted. It has been preached
upon times without number. Who shall say anything new
about it? Who *needs* to say anything new about it? It renews
its youth at every reading; and again at this very moment, as
we turn once more to the gracious words, they break into the
heart with inspiring reassurance.

The circumstances which occasioned these words were
touchingly human, and tinged with something of pathos. In
his poverty and imprisonment, Paul had received a cheering
love-gift from the little church at Philippi far away. His heart
brimmed with appreciation. Maybe the gift was not very much
in terms of Roman coinage; but the Christian love behind it
made it of priceless worth to Paul. He must write them, and
make special mention of their kindness. Thus Philippians iv.
19 is penned in affectionate reciprocation.

But the verse is no mere optative expression of goodwill.
It is an *assurance*. Coming, as it does, from an inspired pen, it
is a God-given pledge to us of the Divine all-sufficiency.

How the terms of this promise gladden the eye of the Christian! That expression, "My God"—how becomingly it flows from the pen of the grand apostle! and how well it befits the lips of Christ's own, whom God has redeemed to be a peculiar treasure to Himself!

Sometimes impious men take this expression upon their lips as a blasphemous oath. This is a terrible thing to do. Let men of such profane mouths beware; for they will presently find it a dreadful thing to fall into the hand of the living God. But the believer can take the words upon his lips and find much sweetness in them; for to him "the God and Father of our Lord Jesus" is "*my* God" in the most blessed sense of the word.

Admittedly there is a sense in which God is "my God" to every human being. In Him we all live and move and have our being; and to Him we must all give account. Paul is far from using the words in this general way. The pronoun "my" is emphatic here. Seven times in this epistle Paul uses this pronoun of himself. He speaks of "my grace" (i. 7), "my hope" (i. 20), "my joy" (ii. 2 and iv. 1), "my Lord" (iii. 8), and "my God" (i. 3 and iv. 19). It is an unusual sort of prisoner who speaks of "my grace," "my hope," "my joy"! Prison, privation, poverty, adversity of any kind, all are sweetened by "grace" and "hope" and "joy" when we can say in the Pauline way, "*my* God."

To the Christian, God has become "my God" in virtue of *covenant relationship*. As God is an infinite, eternal, and immutable Intelligence, it follows that from the beginning He has had formed an all-comprehensive and unchangeable plan of all His works in time, including creation and providence and redemption. Away back in the counsels of the eternal Trinity the Covenant of Grace was formed before the foundation of the world, the Father and the Son being the contracting Parties therein, the Son as the Second Adam representing all His people as Mediator and Surety, assuming their place and undertaking all their obligations. In the mystery and glory of predestinating grace, Christ's blood-bought people have been covenanted to Him by the Father from the eternal ages. Thus we find our Lord saying of His sheep, "*My Father, which gave them Me*, is greater than all, and no man is able to pluck them out of My Father's hand." He says again, addressing the Father (John xvii), "Thine they were, and *Thou gavest them Me.*" It is in virtue of this covenant that the words of God through the prophet became applicable to Christ's people, " I will put my law in their inward parts, and write it in their hearts; and *I will be their God, and they shall be My people.*" He is thus "my God" by a covenant bond.

But further, the Christian may take this appropriating pronoun on his lips as the by-product of an inward *filial relationship* with God. He is "my God" because I am His regenerate child, begotten again to Him in Jesus Christ, and indwelt by the Spirit of adoption. In the words of Galatians iv. 6, "Because we are sons, God hath sent forth the Spirit of His Son into our hearts, crying Abba Father." If the Spirit of God Himself thus witnesses within me that God is my Father and I am His child, then arising from this filial relationship He is indeed "my God" in a most blessed and heartfelt way.

Again, the believer may say He is "my God" as *a proven fact of experience.* Let me but look back over the years. Ah yes, in a thousand ways God has proved Himself to be "my God." When the storm has raged He has flung his mantle round me. When the battle has waxed hot, He has shielded me from the fiery darts of the wicked. He has led me and fed me. He has answered my prayers. He has shown me that underneath me are the everlasting arms of a love which never lets me go, and never gives me up. Full well has He proved himself to be "my God."

He is "my God" because He has "chosen" me in Christ "before the foundation of the world." He is "my God" because *I* have chosen *Him* to be first in my love and in my life; because He has *saved* me; and because I have yielded myself to His service for ever.

> Heaven and earth may fade and flee,
>   First-born light in gloom decline ;
> But while God and I shall be,
>   I am His and He is mine.

If then God is "my God," dare I say anything less than that He will supply all my needs?

Look at the gracious promise in its *connection.* There is a contrastive parallel between the way in which the Philippians had supplied Paul's need, and the way in which God would supply theirs. Paul says, as it were, "*You* have supplied my need: GOD shall supply yours. You have supplied *one* of my needs: God will supply ALL yours. You have supplied me out of your *poverty*: God shall supply you according to His RICHES. You have sent your gift to me by *Epaphroditus*, a true servant of Jesus Christ: God shall supply all your need by CHRIST JESUS HIMSELF."

Look also at the promise in its *construction*. Everything gathers round the one verb "supply," and amplifies it. Thus in this promise we see a seven-fold perfection of supply. Here is—

The source of the supply—"my God."
The certainty of the supply—"shall."
The fulness of the supply—"fulfil" (R.V.).
The extent of the supply—"all your need."
The measure of the supply—"according to His riches."
The storehouse of the supply—"in glory."
The medium of the supply—"in Christ Jesus."

No Christian need ever beg bread with a promise like this in the Bible. We are unkind to ourselves and dishonouring to God when we tantalize ourselves with nervous fears.

Here is the bank—"my God."
Here is the check—"shall supply".
Here is the amount—"all your need."
Here is the capital—"His riches."
Here is the bank address—"in glory."
Here is the signature—"by Christ Jesus."

What then remains for *us* to do? We must put our own signature to it, for no cheque will receive payment at a bank counter, unendorsed. We sign our names to it, and the needed supply is ours.

We need have no fear. That word "*shall*" is too definite for us ever to be let down. C. H. Spurgeon says: "The writer knows what it is to be tried in the work of the Lord. Fidelity has been recompensed with anger, and liberal givers have stopped their subscriptions; but he whom they sought to suppress has not been one penny the poorer, nay, rather he has been the richer; for this promise has been true, 'My God shall supply all your need.' *God's supplies are surer than the Bank of England.*"

Years ago, a dear old Christian woman who lived alone in a village cottage had used her last penny and her last loaf. She knelt at her table and prayed God to supply her with a loaf. Some village youths who often teased her for her religion overheard the prayer, and decided to play a joke by quickly getting a loaf wrapped up and dropping it down the chimney. This they did; and as the dear old woman was rising from her knees, what should she hear and see but a brown parcel come down through the wide old-fashioned chimney! Upon opening the parcel and seeing what was inside, she lifted up her voice in praise to God; but the youths then opened the door and laughingly exclaimed, "Ah, it was we who sent the loaf, and not God at all!" The dear old saint, however, was not to be so easily mocked after all, for she quickly replied, "Dinna ye think it my laddies: God sent it, even if He let the devil bring it!" God may use a variety of agencies, but He will fulfil His promise.

> Say not, my soul, From whence
> Can God relieve my care?
> Remember that Omnipotence
> Has servants everywhere.

The word "*supply*" in this promise means, literally, to fill full. More recent versions read: "My God shall *fulfil* every need of yours." Our need is as it were an empty vessel, and God's supply is that which fills the vessel to the brim. The thought takes our minds back to 2 Kings iv, to the account of the widow and her cruse of oil. The woman is in desperate need. The creditor has come to take her sons as bondmen. She has nothing in the house but a pot of oil. The prophet Elisha says to her, "Go, borrow thee vessels abroad of all thy neighbours, even empty vessels; borrow not a few." This is promptly done. Elisha's further word is, "Thou shalt pour out into all those vessels, and thou shalt set aside that which is full." The woman takes her solitary cruse of oil, and begins to pour out.

There would be small jars, big jars—jars of all shapes and sizes. She comes to one very large container, and thinks, as she glances again at her own small oil-pot, "Why, *this* will never fill *that!*" Yet as she pours, the more there *is* to pour!—until all the receptacles are filled to utmost capacity, and she calls for yet another, only to find that the supply is greater than all that which needed to be filled. Then the oil is sold; the creditor is paid; the sons are set free; and the woman's need is "filled full" even as were the oil-pots, and in a way which becomes for ever a type of how God "supplies," or fills full, the needs of His people.

> Though troubles assail, and dangers afright;
> Though friends should all fail, and foes all unite;
> Yet one thing secures us, whatever betide,—
> The Scripture assures us "The Lord will provide."

Look at the *completeness* of the promised supply—"*all* your need," or, as alternative versions give it, "*every* need of yours." What a vast field this covers!—needs of body, of mind, of spirit; for ourselves and for our families; for the present and for the future; needs as parents, as children, as husbands, as wives, as masters, as servants, as citizens, as sinners, as saints. Our needs are as many as our moments. The greatest tree of the forest, bending beneath its weight of summer foliage, has not a thousandth part as many leaves as we have needs. When we can count the sands of the Sahara we may guess the number of our needs. But God knows *all* our needs; and His supply is both commensurate and constant. This is no mere toying with artificial platitudes: it is glorious truth. Would that the Lord's people put it more to the test, and proved its reality more fully! What a lot of unbelieving believers there are!

Some years ago, Richard Hill, a veteran Christian worker in Glasgow, was informed that a certain Christian man had died. "I hope he had the assurance of an abundant entrance," said Mr. Hill. "Na, na," replied his informant, "he gaed on doubtin' to the end, like a good Presbyterian." O the hang-back doubt that thwarts and cripples thousands of professing Christians to-day! How it dishonours God, and denies the Lord's people their heritage of "joy and peace in believing"!

If our faith were but more simple
We should take Him at His word;
And our lives would be all sunshine
In the sweetness of our Lord.

A godly woman who lived in the days of persecution used
to say that she would never lack because God had promised
to "supply all her need." She was taken before an unjust
judge for attending the worship of God. On seeing her the
judge tauntingly said, "I have often wished to have you in
my power; I shall now send you to prison; and *then* how will
you be fed?" The woman replied, "If it be my heavenly
Father's pleasure, I shall be fed from your own table." It
eventuated that the woman actually was fed from the judge's
own table; for the judge's wife was present at the trial, and
was so impressed by the good woman's faith that she sent food
to her from her own table all through the term of imprisonment!

In some way or other the Lord will provide:
It may not be *my* way;
It may not be *thy* way;
And yet in His own way, the Lord will provide.

Note that it is our "needs" which God pledges to supply.
God could do nothing unkinder to some of us than to say
yes to all our mere "wants." Sometimes, too, even things
which we deem really needful are withholden that we may
become more grateful for the blessings which we already have,
and that we may be led into closer leaning upon God. A
heathen philosopher long ago went into the temple of his
idol-god to complain because he had no shoes. As he rose
from before the idol he saw that the man next to him had *no
feet*. Overcome with rebuke he kneeled down again to give
thanks that he himself had feet. God's denials are often His
choicest benefactions to us; and we may be sure that no real
need will go unsupplied.

See the *measure* of the promised supply: "My God shall
supply all your need *according to His riches*." Who can conceive
the riches of *God*? Let us not waste words trying to describe
the indescribable. His riches, like Himself, are infinite. We
read of "the riches of His goodness," "the riches of His glory,"

"the riches of His wisdom," "the riches of His grace," "the unsearchable riches of Christ."

Now it is not just "out of," but "according to" His riches that God supplies us. There is a big difference between "out of" and "according to." A man who possesses more than ten million dollars is passing down a street one day, when he sees a very poor relative of his. "How are you getting on?" he asks. "Very badly indeed," is the reply. "I don't know where to turn or what to do." The wealthy man says, "I will help you. Here's half a dollar." Half a dollar!—he could have given him ten thousand or more and scarcely felt it! Half a dollar!—he has given "out of" his wealth, but not "according to"!

We do well to note the occurrences of that expression "according to" in God's word. It can teach us a great deal.

In 1 Kings x. we have the Queen of Sheba's visit to King Solomon. In the thirteenth verse, we read, "King Solomon gave unto the queen of Sheba all her desire, whatsoever she asked, beside that which Solomon gave her of his royal bounty." Here are three measures of Solomon's generous giving: (i) "whatsoever she asked," (ii) "all her desire," (iii) "that which Solomon gave her of his royal bounty." There is a striking parallel between this and Ephesians iii. 20 and 21. "Now unto Him that is able to do exceeding abundantly above all that we ask or think." Here is the same threefold measure: (i) "all that we ask," (ii) "all that we think," (iii) "exceeding abundantly above" (Solomon's "royal bounty"!). Thus Israel's richest king, is a type of the heavenly King Who bestows upon us the treasures of *His* riches.

Now the saying that King Solomon gave to the Queen of Sheba "of his royal bounty," is, literally translating the Hebrew, that he gave to her "*according to the hand of king Solomon.*" How eloquently this speaks the lavish bounty which he heaped upon his royal visitor! No king so rich as he!—and he gave to her in a way that corresponded; not "out of" but "according to"! Even so, "My God shall supply all your need *according to* HIS *riches.*"

It will take eternal ages to exhibit all that is meant in that "according to." Indeed, this is stated in the text, for when it says that God will fulfil all our need according to His riches "in glory," it does not mean merely that God's *riches* are "in glory" (which would be a needless redundancy), but that according to His riches He will fill full, or fill *to the point of completion* all our need "in glory." Our present needs are met here and now, for the text includes all these; but our need will be completingly fulfilled *"in glory"*—in the glory yet to be!

Finally: all God's riches, and all the fulfillings of our need, come to us, as the text says, "by (in) Christ Jesus." He is the sphere in which the gracious provisions of God operate and are realised. The expression "in Christ" signifies union with Him by faith. If we are thus "in Christ," Philippians iv. 19 is ours; and while this promise remains we need not fear. When the throne of God collapses, and only then, will this word of grace break down.

See, as soon as Paul has penned this promise, he knows he need say no more, and he winds up his epistle with the following doxology, in which let every Christian heart gratefully join.

"NOW UNTO OUR GOD AND FATHER BE THE GLORY UNTO THE AGES OF THE AGES: AMEN."

Some years ago, away up in a Scottish village-town, there lived a dear old Christian woman commonly known as "Dear old Nancy." She had been bed-ridden for years, but was unchangingly cheery, and full of "the joy of the Lord." She was always speaking or singing about *"the promises"*; and for hours at a time she would revel in looking them up in the pages of God's word, and pondering their meaning. The minister of the local "kirk" was often in to see her, and invariably he felt that he *received* more blessing than he *gave*. He was a truly godly man, and rejoiced in "the promises" as dear old Nancy herself did. But one day he thought he would tease her a little. He said: "Look here, Nancy, every time I come in to see you, it's just the same—you're always talking about 'the promises.' Does it never occur to you that some of the promises might not be true?" For a moment poor old Nancy was thunderstruck. Such a blasphemous suggestion had never dared cross the threshold of her trustful mind. But, quickly recovering herself, and struggling into a sitting posture, she said in tones of awesome seriousness and finality: "What! these promises not true? Never! Why, if these promises are not true, poor old Nancy loses her soul,—and *God loses His character!*" Yes, the very character of God is bound up with the promises.

De Witt Talmage tells of the following incident. There was a man who came over from New York some years ago, and threw himself down on the lounge in his house, and said, "Well, everything's gone." They said, "What do you mean?" "Oh," he replied, "we have had to suspend payment; our house has gone to pieces—nothing left." His little child bounded from the other side of the room, and said, "Papa, you have me left." And the wife, who had been very sympathetic and helpful, came up, and said, "Well, my dear, you have me left." And the old grandmother, seated in a corner of the room, put up her spectacles on her wrinkled forehead, and said, "My son, *you have all the promises of God left.*" Then the merchant burst into tears, and said, "What an ingrate I am! I find I have a great many things left. God, forgive me."

Oh, doubting, fearing soul, all the promises of God are still left to you! The very character of God is bound up with them. And what is true of all of them is true of Philippians iv. 19 in particular. Look at it once again—

"MY GOD SHALL SUPPLY ALL YOUR NEED ACCORDING TO HIS RICHES IN GLORY BY CHRIST JESUS."

MY HEART

In me Thy workmanship display'd,
  A miracle of power I stand;
Fearfully, wonderfully made,
  And framed in secret by Thy hand:
I lived, ere into being brought,
Through Thine eternity of thought.

How precious are Thy thoughts of peace,
  O God, to me! how great the sum!
New every morn, they never cease;
  They were, they are, and yet shall come,
In number and in compass more
Than ocean's sands or ocean's shore.—
                    JAMES MONTGOMERY.

O to grace how great a debtor
  Daily I'm constrained to be!
Let that grace Lord, like a fetter,
  Bind my wandering heart to Thee.
Prone to wander, Lord, I feel it;
  Prone to leave the God I love:
Take MY HEART, O take and seal it,
  Seal it for Thy courts above.—
                    ROBERT ROBINSON.

MY HEART

"Search me, O God, and know my heart; try me, and know my thoughts; and see if there be any wicked way in me; and lead me in the way everlasting.—Ps. cxxxix. 23, 24.

OUR KNOWLEDGE of God gathers itself up in seven foundational and comprehensive terms, three expressing the Divine *nature*, and four expressing the Divine *attributes*.

The Divine Nature.
    "God is spirit" (John iv. 24).
    "God is light" (1 John i. 5).
    "God is love" (1 John iv. 8).

The Divine Attributes.
    God is omnipotent,
        His power is boundless.
    God is omniscient,
        His knowledge is absolute.
    God is omnipresent,
        His presence is everywhere.
    God is triune,
        One nature in three Persons.

There are other vast terms which we employ in referring to the Divine Being, as when we say that God is infinite, unchangeable, eternal; but the infinitude, eternality, and immutability of God are really involved in the seven inclusive terms which we have submitted, as, indeed, are all other conceptions of the nature and mode of the Divine existence.

In this one-hundred-and-thirty-ninth psalm, piety and poetry blend to set forth the Divine nature and attributes in their relation to the individual human heart. The first person singular, "I," "me," "my," goes hand in hand with the second person singular, "Thou," "Thee," "Thy," practically through-out. Until we come to the last few lines of the piece there are but two beings in the universe—God and the psalmist. Nor can any of ourselves to-day read these verses thoughtfully without feeling, as did the psalmist, that God and the soul are looking upon each other in detachment from all else. To read this psalm slowly and meditatively is an enrichment to the soul. We are face to face with the true God, and with ourselves as we really are in His sight. This is the psalm of *God and my own heart*. It is a gem of literature; and, moreover, its lofty conceptions rebuke those who belittle the Old Testament apprehension of Deity and morality.

It is something to be much regretted that the majority of English readers are largely prevented from perceiving the poetic form and literary charm of the psalms, owing to the verse arrangement in our Authorized Version. It is well to read the psalms in the Revised Version, where effort has been made to preserve the thought-rhythm and poetic parallelism. This one-hundred-and-thirty-ninth psalm is a poem, a poem possessing a literary excellence which is equalled only by the majesty and sublimity of its spiritual message. Far from being any mere string of loosely connected verses, it is a methodically constructed composition. Its twenty-four verses are arranged into four strophes of six verses each. In the first six verses we have the Divine omniscience. In the second six verses we have the Divine omnipresence. In the third six verses we have the Divine omnipotence. Then, in the final six verses, we have the reaction of the psalmist himself to these lofty considerations, ending with an earnest prayer. His contemplation of God brings him to his knees in adoration and fervent entreaty. May the psalm have a like effect upon ourselves!

THE DIVINE OMNISCIENCE

Look, then, at the first strophe, running, in our English version, from verse 1 to verse 6. Here I see the absoluteness of the Divine knowledge viewed in relation to myself.

First, in verse 1, I am told that God knows *my character*: "O Lord, Thou hast searched *me*, and known *me*." Then, in verse 2, I am told that God knows *my contemplations*, that is, all my thoughts and purposes: "Thou knowest my downsitting and mine uprising; Thou understandest my thought afar off." Then, in verse 3, I am told that God knows *my conduct*: "Thou compassest my path and my lying down, and art acquainted with all my ways." Yet again, in verse 4, I am told that God knows *my conversation*: "For there is not a word in my tongue, but lo, O Lord, Thou knowest it altogether." Thus God knows me through and through—my character, my contemplations, my conduct, my conversation.

Note the double occurrence of the pronoun "me" in the first verse of the psalm: "O Lord, Thou hast searched me, and known *me*." It will be observed that in our English version the second "me" is in italics. This is because it does not occur here in the Hebrew, which reads, "O Lord, Thou hast searched me, and known . . ." There is some kind of an ellipsis here. Instead of repeating the "me," ought we not to read it "my heart"? To read it thus preserves the thought-balance of the stanza, according to the style of the poetry, and makes a true parallel between the opening sentence of the psalm and the prayer at the end of the last strophe, where we have again the "me" and the "my heart"—"Search me, O God, and know my heart." Reading the first verse thus, we see even more clearly the sequence and completeness of the first four verses, speaking, as they do, of heart, thoughts, deeds, words.

MY HEART "O Lord, Thou hast searched me, and known my heart" (v. 1).

MY THOUGHT "Thou understandest my thought afar off" (v. 2).

MY ACTIONS "Thou . . . art acquainted with all my ways" (v. 3).

MY WORDS "Not a word in my tongue, but Thou knowest it altogether" (v. 4).

This covers the whole moral man, the whole of our inner and outer life. The Divine omniscience is here gazed on, not as a mere theological or philosophical abstraction, but as a tremendous reality realizedly bearing upon my whole life and being, from the inmost spring of my personality even to the commonest words of my daily converse. We do not wonder that the inspired poet, subdued, should feel, and say, "Thou has beset me behind and before, and laid Thine hand upon me. Such knowledge is too wonderful for me; it is high, I cannot attain unto it" (vv. 5 and 6).

The reality of this inescapable, unrelaxing, unforgetting scrutiny of an all-seeing Eye is a torture to the ungodly man whenever he dares to think upon it. What are the grasshopper scientists of earth compared with this omnipotent *Omni-scientist*, this all-penetrating Mental Analyst, this absolutely infallible Psychologist, who sees, and knows, and sifts, and weighs, and reads, and understands all His creatures through and through? It is a fearful thing indeed for the hypocrite and the impenitent transgressor to fall into the hand of this living and all-seeing God! This is a truth which surely needs charging home upon the scornful sinners of to-day, who think by the denial of God's existence to shield themselves from the discomfort of God's acknowledged presence. They cannot escape this omniscient King and Judge of the universe. One awful day they must be brought to book, unless they come to know the saving grace of God in Christ; and it is our solemn duty to warn them, despite their derisive, pretended incredulity, lest at last their blood should be upon our own garments.

To the sincere Christian, however, washed in the precious blood of the Saviour, raised to newness of life by the regenerating Spirit, and conscientiously walking in the will of God, this truth of the Divine omniscience is a source of much comfort. The renewed and sincere heart may be misunderstood, misjudged, and made to suffer by men; but it rejoices to fall back on this consolation, that an all-seeing and all-knowing God is its righteous and final Vindicator. Yea, how the true believer prizes this truth of the all-seeing One! The very One who thus sees and knows us is the God of Calvary. Much of our human love is based on a partial ignorance of the object loved; but there is One who knows the inmost and utmost about us, and yet loves us with a love that is stronger than death.

> Come and rejoice with me,
> For I have found a Friend
> Who knows my heart's most secret depths,
> Yet loves me without end!

Some of the terms here used to describe God's knowledge of us are arresting. That word "searched" indicates a process of minute investigation, a searching out as when one is bent on finding hidden treasures or secrets. The word "known" indicates the *result* of this penetrating investigation in complete knowledge. The expression, "understandest my thoughts afar off," implies that God observes and discerns all the thought processes in the intricate mechanism of the mind, and sees our thoughts as they evolve from the indefinitely subconscious to the clearly and definitely conscious. How can we but wonder at such knowledge, and say with the psalmist, "Such knowledge is too wonderful for me; it is high, I cannot attain unto it"? This, then, is the first overwhelming thought here regarding the relationship between God and the individual soul, that God completely knows the whole man.

THE DIVINE OMNIPRESENCE

Look, now, at the second strophe, covering the second six of the verses as given in our Authorised Version. David asks, "Whither shall I go from Thy Spirit? or whither shall I flee from Thy presence (lit.—from Thy face)"? The psalm clearly shows, of course, that David did not ask this question because he *wished* to escape God's presence, but in order to show the impossibility of doing so; and in showing the utter absurdity of attempting to elude God he resorts in imagination to five extremes.

First, there is the extreme of *height*: "If I ascend up into heaven Thou art there." David knows full well that he cannot scale the measureless ascent, or stand amid that blinding glory; but by a soaring flight of imagination he rises to the highest heaven, only to find that any endeavouring to escape God there is like flying into the centre of the sun to avoid its heat.

Next, there is the extreme of *depth*: "If I make my bed in Sheol, behold, Thou art there!" As the heaven of heavens, the special abode of God, was considered to be the highest height, so the abyss of Sheol, the place of the wicked departed, was conceived to be the deepest depth—as indeed it *is* for the impenitent, in a real and awful sense. Surely God shall be escaped *there*! Nay (note David's exclamation of surprise) "*Behold*, Thou art there!" Whatever Sheol may be, and whoever may be there, *God* is there. His presence may have an effect as awful there as it is glorious in heaven; but the fact is that He *is* there. He fills the heights of heaven. He fills the depths of hell.

Again, there are the two extremes of *East and West*: "If I take the wings of the morning, (if I) dwell in the uttermost parts of the sea . . ." This elegant image, "the wings of the morning," is a poetic reference to the sunrise, and, therefore, to the east. In Palestine, except during the brief seasons of the early and latter rains, clouds appear only at sunrise; but these silvery-white, opal-tinted, wing-like clouds of the early morning often make an exquisitely beautiful picture. Says James Neil: "By about seven o'clock the heat has dissipated these fleecy clouds, and to the vivid eastern imagination Morn has folded her outstretched wings." David's further figure—"the uttermost parts of the sea"—sweeps us out to the farthest reaches of the west, away across the Mediterranean, which is the "sea" spoken of here. The great sea was always the west to the old-time Israelite. Extreme east, or extreme west, it makes no difference, "Even there shall Thy hand lead me, and Thy right hand shall hold me."

Finally, there is the extreme of *darkness*: "If I say: Surely the darkness shall cover me . . ." Dense darkness is considered to be the securest of all coverings. Wherever a man may hide in the daytime, he can be seen if any should chance that way; but the darkness is such a screen as no mortal eye can see through, so that a man may say, with emphasis, "*Surely* the darkness shall cover me." Yet will even this hide from God? Nay, is not darkness itself a thing of God's creating for the tired eyes of mortal man? It is a thing which God has related to the physical eye of the creature, but it is no curtain to the spiritual eye of God. We may sin in broad daylight just as well as at midnight so far as hiding from God is concerned. "If I say: Surely the darkness shall cover me, even the night shall be light about me: yea, the darkness hideth not from Thee, but the night shineth as the day; the darkness and the light are both alike to Thee."

> Darkness and light in this agree,
> Great God, they're both alike to Thee.
> Thine hand can pierce Thy foes as soon
> Through midnight shades as blazing noon.

This, then, is the second strophe. It is great poetry; but far greater than the poetry is the awe-inspiring reality. As an omniscient God knows us through and through, so an omnipresent God is with us always and everywhere. A heathen philosopher once asked, "Where is God?" A Christian believer replied: "Let me first ask you: Where is He not?" His universal immanence is as real and tremendous as his infinite transcendence.

The omnipresence of God, like the omniscience of God, is a frightful thought to the evil-doer. Well may the workers of ill and the lovers of darkness cringe beneath this sword which hangs above their necks! We may outwit the vigilance of a human foe, but we can never elude Him in whom we live and move and have our being. We may out-distance a human enemy; but we can never place ourselves beyond the reach of Him who fills the universe. We may out-bide the ability of an earthly adversary to strike us, for often the power of men declines with the lapse of years; but we can never outbide the One who fills the ages and has all eternity in which to strike. We may outlive a mortal foe, for death may cut him down and remove him from us; but the eternal One is an Avenger who never dies. We ourselves may die before an earthly hand can fell us, and thus death, coming to ourselves, may keep an earthly foe from smiting us; but even death cannot bear us away from God, for though we make our bed in Sheol, behold, God is there! Oh, this dread truth of the Divine omnipresence—well may it strike consternation into the breast that harbours sin!

Certainly the omnipresence of God should come as a salutary consideration to all thoughtful men and women. The famous botanist, Linnæus, was so impressed with it that he had the words written over his library door, *Innocui vivite, Numen adest* —"Live innocently, Deity is present." There is a great influence, both to restrain from vice and to constrain toward chastity, in the thought of the Divine omnipresence. Looking back over his travels abroad in younger years, Milton wrote: "I again take God to witness that in all places where so many things are considered lawful, I lived sound and untouched from profligacy and vice, having this thought perpetually with me, that though I might escape the eyes of men, I certainly could not the eyes of God." As another has said, "If the presence of a good man or woman, or someone we love, or of a little child, often restrains, so that though tempted sorely we cannot yield, how much more the realised presence of God? As we go about our daily life, let us halt often, and say, 'God is now here,' say it in every time of temptation, sometimes adding this other word, 'Thou has set our secret sins in the light of Thy countenance.'"

But, again, the reality of the all-pervading immanence of God is a source of unspeakable consolation to the godly. David himself found satisfaction in the thought, as the psalm shows. Confronted by difficulties, surrounded by foes, dogged by adversities, the Christian replenishes his courage in this, that God Himself is sympathetically and sustainingly with him all the time and in every place. Far from home and kindred, ploughing a lonely furrow, treading a deserted path, fighting a lonely battle, far removed maybe, from familiar and beloved haunts, the Christian leans on this unfailing staff of assurance, "Fear thou not, for I am with thee." Ah, thank God, there are no boundaries to the Divine presence and keeping power.

> I know not where His islands lift
>   Their fronded palms in air;
> I only know I cannot drift
>   Beyond His love and care.

To lovers, separation is pain, and to be in each other's presence is happiness. So is it with the true Christian and his Divine Lord; there is no sweeter thought than this, that nothing can ever hide us from our Lord's unslumbering eye, or separate us from His boundless presence.

> Thy children shall not faint nor fear—
> Sustained by this delightful thought,
> Since Thou, our God, art everywhere,
> We cannot be where Thou art not.

THE DIVINE OMNIPOTENCE

We come now to the third strophe, the third group of six verses in our English Bible, verses 13 to 18. Here with strokes of delicate skill, the royal poet speaks concerning the mystery of human birth and life, beholding in man the crown of creative achievement, the product, and at the same time the *evidence*, of the Divine omnipotence.

The subject and language of verses 13 to 16 are of such a sacred and delicate nature as to be more suited to private reading. Adam Clark wisely observes, "We are taught by the peculiar delicacy of expression in the Sacred Writings to avoid, as in this case, the entering too minutely into anatomical details." The psalmist, in pondering the complex wonder of human being and personality, finds himself treading back with awed steps to the mystery of the prenatal state. We would merely point out the five verbs which the psalmist uses here to express this marvel of Divine power.

In verse 13 the two verbs, "possessed," and "covered," referring to the embryonic stage, ought to be read as "formed" and "woven." In verse 14, the expression "wonderfully made" means *separated*, or *set apart*, probably referring to birth itself. In verse 15 we have the two verbs, "made" and "curiously wrought," the latter meaning *wrought like embroidery*. None can consider these five verbs, "formed," "woven," separated," "fashioned," "skilfully wrought," in their connection, without marvelling at the mystery of human life and at the power of God.

Some of the terms which the psalmist uses in this passage express with remarkable vividness the wonder of the constitution; but we must leave them. The complexity, delicacy, intricacy, and exquisite mechanism of the human system are such as to inspire us with a sensation of awe. It has been said that if we could see one half of what is going on within us we would scarcely dare to move! Who can study even a model of our anatomy without feelings of amazement? Who can dissect any part of the human frame without wondering at its delicacy, and trembling at its frailty? Veins, sinews, muscles, nerves—what tapestry can match the human fabric? Eyes, ears, bones, limbs, organs, arteries—what edifice can vie with such

architecture as we have here? Matter, mind, motion, thought
volition, affection, aspiration, psycho-physical union and
interaction as mysterious as it is exquisitely balanced and
sensitive—what marvel of modern invention shall we dare put
alongside *this* marvel?

> Our life contains a thousand springs,
>   And dies if one be gone:
> Strange that a harp of thousand strings
>   Should keep in tune so long!

But the psalmist has another thing to tell us. In verse 16
he says, "In thy book all my members were written, which
in continuance were fashioned, when as yet there was none of
them." The Hebrew more literally runs thus:

> And in Thy book all were written:
> The days (that) were formed,
>   When yet there was not one of them.

This would make it seem that it is the "days" and not the
"members," which were written beforehand in God's book.
If we take the marginal reading of the Hebrew, a still more
striking word confronts us: "And for it (that is, for the birth
of the embryo) there was one (day) among them (predestined
in God's book)." But whether it be the "members," or the
"days," or *the* "day," what can be more impressively declared
the omnipotence of God than this foreknowledge and fore-
determining with regard to individual human birth and life?

We do not wonder that the psalmist should exclaim, "I
am fearfully and wonderfully made: marvellous are thy
works; and that my soul knoweth right well!" David is no
isolated figure as he stands marvelling at the mystery and
majesty of the creative skill which God displays in the origin-
ating and perpetuating of man. Millions of David's fellow
creatures have likewise stood in adoring awe before this same
wonder, and have bowed in worship before such a God.

Not long ago, writing in the columns of a newspaper and describing the vastness of the universe as known to modern astro-
nomy, a leading British scientist asked rather despisingly:
"Astronomically speaking, what is *man*?" A reader replied, begging to inform him that "astronomically speaking" man is the
astronomer! At the first God said, "Let us make man in Our

image." That is more than suns, than stars, than all the vast, revolving systems of mere matter. Truly, as the psalmist here realizes, if God can make man, He can make anything. Says the poet Edward Young:

> How poor, how rich, how abject, how august,
> How complicate, how wonderful is man!
> How passing wonder He who made him such,
> Who centred in our make such strange extremes!
> From different natures marvellously mixed,
> Connexion exquisite of distant worlds!
> Distinguished link in being's endless chain!
> Midway from nothing to the Deity!
> A beam, ethereal, sullied and absorbed!
> Though sullied and dishonoured, still divine!
> Dim miniature of greatness absolute!
> An heir of glory, a frail child of dust!
> Helpless immortal, insect infinite!
> A worm! a god!—I tremble at myself,
> And in myself am lost! At home a stranger,
> Thought wanders up and down, surprised, aghast,
> And wondering at her own: how reason reels!
> O what a miracle to man is man!

As we think of the power, the thought, the love, the care, which God exercises toward man, toward *men*, toward each of us, do we not find ourselves speaking words akin to those with which the psalmist closes this third strophe?—"How precious, also, are Thy thoughts unto me, O God! How great is the sum of them! If I should count them, they are more in number than the sand. When I awake, I am still with Thee."

THE HUMAN REACTION

The Revised rendering of the final strophe runs as follows:

> Surely Thou wilt slay the wicked, O God;
> Depart from me therefore, ye bloodthirsty men.
> For they speak against Thee wickedly,
> And thine enemies take Thy name in vain.
> Do not I hate them, O Lord, that hate Thee?
> And am not I grieved with those that rise up against
>   Thee?
> I hate them with perfect hatred;
> I count them mine enemies.
> Search me, O God, and know my heart;
> Try me, and know my thoughts:
> And see if there be any way of wickedness in me,
> And lead me in the way everlasting.

Here, finally, we see the psalmist's reaction to the sublime qualities and attributes which he has been contemplating. He has gazed with wide-opened eye upon the Divine omniscience, omnipresence, and omnipotence. He has recognised the *spirituality* of God involved in these attributes, clearly expressing this in such words as "Whither shall I go from Thy Spirit? or whither shall I flee from Thy presence?" He has perceived, also, the *love* of God, in the tender forethought and minute care exercised toward the individual human creature, as we see in such words as "How precious, also, are Thy thoughts unto me, O God! how great is the sum of them! If I should count them, they are more in number than the sand." Now, further, he thinks on the awful *holiness* of this God, and exclaims (as the more literal rendering goes), "Oh, if Thou wouldst smite the wicked, O God! And ye men of violence, depart from me, who rebel against Thee with wicked deeds, and lift up against Thee vainly."

A man cannot truly know and love God without making a clean break with sin; for when sin is viewed in the light of the Divine character its real ugliness is exposed; and when God, this ineffably glorious God, is loved, sin becomes an intolerable enormity. The man who knows and loves God will have nothing in common with evildoers. "What fellowship hath righteousness with unrighteousness? and what communion hath light with darkness? and what concord hath Christ with Belial? and what part hath he that believeth with an infidel? and what agreement hath the temple of God with idols?" A man's attitude to God always determines the haunts he frequents and the company he keeps.

But the psalmist is far too real with God and with himself merely to cry out against sin in others. He will not condemn it in his neighbour while he condones it in himself. The man who knows and loves God will certainly hate sin in others, but he will hate it most of all in himself. Thus we find David turning in upon his own heart again, in the prayer with which the psalm ends. All through his meditation he has been face to face with God, in isolation from all others. He has considered the Divine omniscience, omnipresence, omnipotence, spirituality, and love, all as related *to himself*; and now, as he suddenly realises afresh the awful holiness of God, and breaks forth against the evil-doers around him, he must needs call for the piercing ray to be turned in upon his own inner life: "Search *me*, O God, and know *my* heart; try *me*, and know *my* thoughts; and see if there be any wicked way in *me*; and lead *me* in the way everlasting."

David's contemplation of God brings him to his knees in prayer. This is what should happen with ourselves. Can we live in the light of such a Presence without being in a continual inward attitude of worship and communion?—and is there anything which more than this makes for chaste behaviour and nobility of character? Do not the divine attributes themselves suggest prayer? The omniscience of God suggests the *why* of prayer, that is, we are coming to One whose knowledge and wisdom are perfect. The omnipotence of God suggests the *how* of prayer, that is, we are to pray believingly, for we are coming to One who is "able to do exceeding abundantly." The omnipresence of God suggests the *where*, or the place, of prayer, that is, "in all places whithersoever thou goest," for we are praying to One whose presence has no bounds. In these attributes of God we see the wisdom and power and reach of prayer; and are we not constrained to cry out, with the first disciples, "Lord, teach us to pray"?

But again, David's contemplation of God occasions earnest examination of his *inner life*. He welcomes, even implores, what most men shun with shame and fear—the bringing to light of the inmost and deepest within him. The investigation is to be *intense*: "Search," "know," "try," "see"—these are the terms in which he asks for the piercing scrutiny of the holy God to penetrate his moral being. The investigation is also to be *thorough*: "Me," "my heart," "my thoughts," "my ways"— this is deep and exhaustive. "See if there be *any* way of perversity in me." It is only a sincere man who speaks thus. O what a blessing is such honest dealing with God and ourselves! We call ourselves Christians, we profess godliness, we presumably represent the cause of God and truth in the earth, yet what cages of unclean birds, what dens of reptiles, what pestilential swamps of depravity, are some of these hearts! What pride, what self-choosing, what selfishness and touchiness, what subtle relish of the unholy, what secret compromise, what covered indulgence in unloving and unlovely thoughts, what camouflage and millionfold hypocrisy! It is toleration of these things in the heart which robs prayer of its thrill and glory, makes God seem unreal, mars character, and prevents the saving grace of God from flowing through us to bless others. Sin cannot survive such treatment as David here metes it. One hour of honest dealing with God, in the place of heartsearching prayer, does more to chasten the mind and ennoble the character than all the New Year resolutions and spasmodic resolves of a lifetime. God bring us there!—bring us there daily!—cause us to dwell there always! It may be painful and humbling at first, but we shall discover a secret of power and peace and purity and joy which will be dear to us as life itself.

The closing sentence of the psalm is "*Lead me in the way everlasting.*" Ah, yes, when we really think upon God as David did, when we bring our lives into the light of his face, when we see ourselves as *he* sees us, life is invested with bigger meaning, and we feel our need of *guidance*, of that guidance which only God himself can give. These hearts of ours are prone to stray; they have strayed repeatedly and grievously in the past; they are easily side-tracked, and there are many deceiving influences around us which would draw us off into ways of sorrow.

"Lead me in the way everlasting"—that is, the way that leads to the eternal life and glory of heaven. God's gracious and complete and final answer to this cry is THE LORD JESUS CHRIST. *He* is the Way, the Truth, the Life. He is the Way, to tread. He is the Truth, to trust. He is the Life, to treasure. Without the Way there is no going. Without the Truth there is no knowing. Without the Life there is no growing. Christ is the Way, by which *we* come to *God*. Christ is the Truth, by which *God* comes to *us*. Christ is the Life, by which we live in God and God lives in us. God's way to everlasting life and glory is, in a word, the yielding up of our lives, in unreserved and life-long committal, to the Lord Jesus. It is this full consecration to Christ which makes real in our lives the daily leading of the Holy Spirit. God incline our hearts toward Himself, bringing us to the place of honest heart-searching in His presence, washing us in the cleansing blood of Calvary, refining us by the fire of Pentecost, guiding us by the Holy Spirit, in the way everlasting, and proving to us that God Himself, known and loved and possessed in Jesus Christ, and

flooding the heart with His presence by the Holy Spirit, is
unutterable love and blessedness!

Search me, O God, my actions try,
  And let my life appear
As seen by Thine all-searching eye;
  My heart and ways make clear.

Search all my sense, and know my heart,
  Who only canst make known;
Yea, let the inmost, deepest part
  To me be clearly shown.

Throw light into the darkened cells,
  Where passion reigns within;
Quicken my conscience till it feels
  The loathsomeness of sin.

Search all my thoughts, the secret springs,
  The motives that control;
The chambers where polluted things
  Hold empire o'er my soul.

Search till Thy fiery gaze has cast
  Its holy light through all,
And I by grace am brought at last
  Before Thy face to fall.

Thus prostrate, I shall learn of Thee
  What now I dimly prove,
That Thou, my God, in Christ canst be
  UNUTTERABLE LOVE!